Living and working
in **Dubai**

Pippa Sanderson

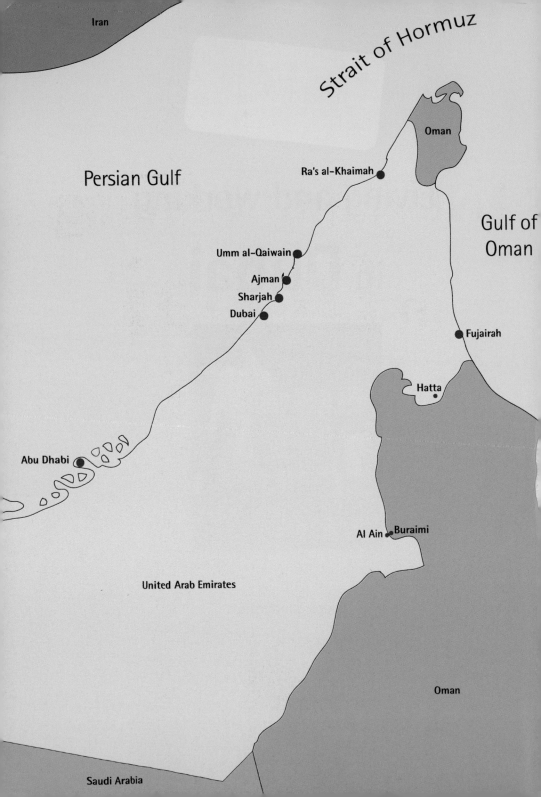

Living and working
in **Dubai**

PYJAMA
PUBLISHING

Published by Pyjama Publishing

PO Box 126, Lymm, Cheshire. WA13 0WE
T: +44 (0) 1925 751467
E: books@pyjamapublishing.com
W: www.pyjamapublishing.com

© 2007 Pippa Sanderson

The author asserts the moral right to be identified as the author of this work.

All photographs by the author, except inside back cover and page 42 top and bottom (Paula Le Flohic); and page 141 bottom (Graham Park).

ISBN: 978 0 9553396 0 8

A CIP catalogue record for this book is available from the British Library.

Printed by Lavenham Press.

Please read the Disclaimer on page 255.

INTRODUCTION

There are many books about Dubai, detailing everything from the city's phenomenal rise from pauper to prince in just a few decades, and the glitz and glamour on offer to the holidaymaker in glossy coffee-table splendour, to the celebration of the wisdom of Dubai's leaders.

There are also one or two books for history buffs and new residents, such as *From Trucial States to United Arab Emirates* by Dr Frauke Heard-Bey, a weighty tome that's widely regarded as offering a true account of the country's history, and Explorer Publishing's *Dubai Explorer*, a guide that encompasses everything from how to get a driving licence to the best bars in town. But there's nothing in the market to give a prospective expatriate an in-depth guide about what it's really like to live and work in this Arabian phenomenon; one of the fastest-growing cities in the world today.

This book attempts to fill this gap by offering a different, yet impartial, perspective that not only highlights the city's many positive aspects but, uniquely, all its aspects, so that, should you decide to make Dubai your home, you do so with your eyes truly open to its many wonders and woes.

To provide objectivity, case studies have been obtained from Dubai residents, many of whom still live in the emirate. In addition, you'll find top tips that should keep you out of trouble, along with a currency converter on page 256.

WINTER HOLIDAY HEAVEN

But first, if you're after a holiday of sun, sea, sand and surf, with plenty of options for refined wining and dining, or simple fare, this truly cosmopolitan,

The Beach Road in Jumeirah, with the high rises of Sheikh Zayed Road in the distance.

Above: General Sheikh Mohammed bin Rashid Al Maktoum, architect of modern Dubai.
Right: Construction of the world's tallest tower – the Burj Dubai – is under way.

safe city fits the bill . . . with plenty of room to spare. You can also be assured of superb entertainment, whether at a bar or at the theatre.

Dubai enjoys more than 300 days of sunshine a year. Winters are glorious, with low humidity and daytime temperatures hovering at the 30°C mark (18°C at night). But summers are hideous, with unofficial temperatures regularly exceeding 50°C during the day. Accompanying high humidity (90 per cent and beyond on occasion) makes for a very unpleasant experience if you happen to venture outside. Even during a summer's night, temperatures rarely dip below 30°C.

Dubai boasts superb beaches, world-class hotels, a limitless, eclectic, cosmopolitan range of restaurants and infinite shopping options, from the Mall of the Emirates, one of the largest shopping malls in the world, and Souk Madinat Jumeirah, a recreation of traditional Arabia, to the real thing at the Gold Souk in Deira, and the forever-popular Karama Market, a long strip of Asian outlets selling everything from souvenirs, clothes and shoes, to fake watches, bags and DVDs.

The holidaymaker can experience the emirate's varied topography by boarding a bus or a dhow (a traditional sailing vessel) for a tour of the city, or a 4x4 for bumping through the desert, dry wadi (river) bed or mountain. They can also immerse themselves in a true Arabian experience of moonlit Arabian desert barbecues, belly dancers and *shisha* (water pipe) smoking.

Where else in the world can you enjoy the surreal incongruity of skiing on real snow inside the Middle East's only indoor ski slope one minute and, bikini-clad, hurtling down the Jumeirah Sceirah at 80 kph at the Wild Wadi water park, or swimming in the warm waters of the Persian Gulf, the next?

More and more people are becoming aware of this slice of Arabia through its exposure on the world stage, along with the intense global marketing efforts of the Department of Tourism and Commerce Marketing (DTCM) and Emirates airline, which, with a seemingly bottomless pit of money at their disposal, have been able to enthuse and extol the virtues of the city without restraint for several years. In this city of the moment, nothing seems impossible. Ongoing developments include the construction of the world's tallest building, the Burj Dubai, along with one of the world's largest shopping malls; massive residential projects, including Dubai Marina, Jumeirah Beach Residence, Dubai Festival City, Dubai Business Bay, the Palm islands and The World; a new railway network and Dubailand, the government's US$5 billion tourism mega-project and the region's answer to Disneyland, which will cover an area of some 115 square kilometres.

The city has made a huge impact on the global leisure and tourism sector, so much so that it's included in the calendars of many sporting events, including the European Tour's Dubai Desert Classic golf tournament, which attracts top golfers such as Tiger Woods and Ernie Els; and the Dubai Open Tennis Championships, which plays host to Roger Federer and Lindsay Davenport among others.

In addition, Dubai has attracted performances from many top entertainers, including Robbie Williams, Destiny's Child, Sir Elton John, Phil Collins, José Carreras and Luciano Pavarotti.

THE NUTS AND BOLTS

Dubai is one of seven emirates that make up the United Arab Emirates (UAE), a country founded in December 1971. Covering an area of some 83,600 square kilometres across the Arabian Peninsula, the country consists of Abu Dhabi, the largest emirate and the location of the nation's capital; Dubai, the second-largest emirate at some 3,885 square kilometres, Sharjah, Ajman, Umm al-Qaiwain, Ra's al-Khaimah and Fujairah. With the city spanning little more than 50 kilometres from end to end, you certainly don't have to go far to find everything you'll ever need within a stone's throw.

The Tedad Census, published in 2006, reveals that the UAE's population stands at just over 4.1 million, with the population of Dubai, 1.2 million. The majority hail from Asia, while UAE nationals account for just 20.1 per cent of the population.

Despite being the minority in their own country, nationals of Dubai strive to maintain their traditional identity in the face of stiff competition from external forces. One obvious sign of this is in the national dress, which is worn by most UAE nationals of both sexes. The men wear a long, usually white ankle-length dress called a *kandoura*, or *dishdash* (although in the winter you'll see various colours from brown, blue, yellow and black), and, typically, a white, or red and white, headdress, called a *gutra*, held in place by a black woollen rope called an *igal*. Undergarments consist of a white skirt, known as a *wazar*, and a white T-shirt.

National women wear a long-sleeved black outer dress, or cape, called an *abaya*, often decorated with sequins while, underneath, the young are dressed in the latest fashions. Heads are covered with a scarf called a *shayla*, which seems to need constant adjustment. Some women also wear a thin veil, a *gishwa*, over their noses, while others cover their entire faces, including their eyes . . . even when driving. Many of the older generation wear a stiff mask covering their mouths, which is known as a *burqa*.

The language of the land is Arabic, although English ranks alongside, especially in business, and is spoken by most . . . to varying degrees.

Islam is the country's official religion and, although the UAE Constitution allows for religious freedom, Article 322 of the Federal Penal Code states that any person caught promoting any religion other than Islam without permission faces a jail term of not less than a year, or a fine of not less than Dhs5,000.

This law was brought into sharp focus by daily newspaper, *Gulf News*, which reported the arrest of two American women, aged 74 and 55, in Dubai in February 2005 for illegally promoting Christianity in public by distributing Bibles. Following questioning, they were bailed and released; and left the country soon afterwards. A source told the newspaper that the police had seized 19 Bibles and 26 CDs.

Above: Dubai's main artery, Sheikh Zayed Road, runs between Abu Dhabi, Dubai and Sharjah.
Below: Sheikh Zayed Road, with the construction of Dubai Business Bay in the foreground.

Dubai Creek, with the elegant National Bank of Dubai building in the centre, the Dubai Chamber of Commerce and Industry building on the right and Etisalat's globe on the left.

The newspaper also referred to a similar incident in 2003, where an elderly Philippino pastor, caught giving an open-air sermon in Ra's al-Khaimah, was convicted of promoting Christianity without obtaining permission, and sentenced to a year in jail. Although the clergyman had official permission to preach inside a church, he was unaware the authorisation did not extend outside. However, the courts handed down a suspended sentence in consideration of the man's age.

According to DTCM's website, "nationals of 'Israel' may not enter the UAE." So resolute is this ban that the British Passport Office has been known to issue second passports to Dubai-resident Britons wishing to visit Israel, so that Israeli entry/exit stamps don't appear in the same passport as that containing a Dubai residence visa.

THE HYPE

Dubai has been a huge PR success. While effectively distancing itself from the fundamentalist/terrorist stereotype with which the Middle East has, for some, become labelled, especially post-9/11, it has been able to present itself as a moderate, liberal enclave of peace and prosperity.

In recognising its supplies of oil were finite (reserves are estimated to run dry by 2010), Dubai has sought to invest in opportunities that reduce its dependence on the black gold. As such, it's wooed the world by creating an infrastructure that's esoteric, eccentric, practical, foolish and incredible; an infrastructure that wholly embraces concepts whose origins can be traced to the REM sleep of some of the world's most creative architects.

Yet while the infrastructures of London, Singapore, Paris and New York have evolved organically over centuries, in parallel with the maturing mindset of the cities' inhabitants, Dubai's petrodollars have been used to create a 21st-century infrastructure in mere decades; in fact you'll find nearly 25 per cent of the world's cranes – some 30,000 – dotting Dubai's cityscape.

Unfortunately, it's inevitable the city's mindset will take some years to catch up with its infrastructure. The resulting incongruity and imbalance has, for many, been extremely difficult to reconcile, especially by new arrivals who, dazzled by the city's fantastic infrastructure, expect too much from a city whose attitudes have a long way to go to match their own.

So ubiquitous is this mindset that many long-term expatriates, some of whom have lived in Dubai since the 1970s (and before), have ceased to evolve from the day they first stepped off the plane or boat; and many have, in fact, regressed to such an extent that, if they were to return to their home countries, the culture shock would be untenable. This is both exacerbated and perpetuated by an attitude of "Well if you don't like it . . . leave", a point of view that allows for no dissention, no challenge to the status quo and no evolution, which has ultimately led to the perception of Dubai being a city of transience.

In 2006, General Sheikh Mohammed bin Rashid Al Maktoum, the Ruler of Dubai and the country's Prime Minister and Vice-President, a keen poet, published a book: *My Vision – Challenges on the Road to Excellence*, in Arabic and English (the author was part of the team editing the translated English text).

Now required reading in all secondary schools, according to the *Gulf News*, Sheikh Mohammed reveals his vision for Dubai to reach the status of the world's most powerful cities and outrun them in every aspect and at all cost; and lead the world in the race towards globalisation. His plans also seek to empower UAE nationals to take over certain roles currently undertaken by non-nationals and, as such, expatriates might be wise to consider Dubai a short-term sojourn, a dip of the toe into a different culture and mindset. To reinforce this attitude, officials at the Ministry of Labour told the United Nations in mid-2006 that expatriates in the UAE should not be regarded as immigrants, but rather as temporary workers who return home after their work contract expires.

FREEING THE PRESS

Dubai's press, at one time, was perceived as being strictly controlled; the emirate's residents cocooned in blissful ignorance. Yet the UAE Constitution allows for freedom of expression, a right endorsed by Sheikh Mohammed, the driving force behind the emirate's rapid development. Indeed, during a speech at the launch of Dubai Media City in November 2000, Sheikh Mohammed said: "I guarantee freedom of expression to all and the right to be completely objective in views and reporting." To drive home this message further, he told journalists a month or so later: "Write what you want to on any issue and on any subject and, as long as you have the proof that whatever you have written is correct, I will be on your side."

With this encouragement, many local journalists and their publishers have been able to nudge the envelope further than ever before by reporting less than favourable items of news. For example, local newspaper *7DAYS* reported that a UAE national was jailed for a month and fined Dhs3,000 in 2006 for, not only being drunk, but insulting two members of the ruling family during a row with his wife.

Much information contained within this book has been gleaned from these local newspapers. When viewed in isolation, these anecdotes mean little but, when woven together in one publication, they create an interesting pattern of attitudes and behaviour that should give you some indication as to the psyche of Dubai's residents. As for the veracity of the newspaper reports, that's up to you to decide.

However, as much as Sheikh Mohammed tries to prise publishers from their comfort zones, many find it easier to remain in safe harbour than navigate such uncharted waters. For example, self-censorship is common, along with the sending of new book and magazine titles to the Ministry of Information's Censorship Department, prior to publication, to ensure a consistent message. Not only that, some 140 Arabic, 380 English, 455 Indian and 40 French newspapers, magazines, books, films, CDs, DVDs and software entering the country have to pass through the 14-man Media Censorship Unit at Dubai Cargo Village before hitting the shelves, resulting in many features, quizzes and photographs bearing too much flesh being either ripped out or scribbled over with heavy black ink.

LAMB DRESSED AS MUTTON

Dubai is a study in *nouveau riche*: vulgar and opulent. For many, it is a master of the opaque, of smoke and mirrors, and is perceived as having little regard for fair play. Someone once said that: "The difference between Dubai and Disney World is that Disney World knows it's a fantasy".

Dubai is also the land of great opportunities where almost anything's possible if you have the get-up-and-go to get it done. Where one person's plan might fail, another's will succeed if he or she knows the right people.

There are seldom any boundaries with what can and can't be done, but laws are ambiguous, non-existent and not seen to be enforced so, in the ensuing confusion, it's often best to try something and later apologise for it if it's wrong, rather than not try it at all.

On a final note, although you'll read the, sometimes harsh, realities of living and working in Dubai within this book, please do keep in mind that many people still enjoy a great time in the emirate (and have no wish to leave). One major plus point is that if you do decide to move to Dubai, you'll meet an eclectic, friendly mix of people, from all walks of life; find you have much in common and gain friends for life.

Above: The majority of Dubai's population hail from Asia, while UAE nationals are the country's minority group.
Right: Construction workers receive a briefing at the site of the Dubai International Financial Centre.

Above and right: The opulence of the Burj Al Arab, the world's only, unofficial, seven-star hotel.

HISTORY

The history of Dubai can be traced back several thousand years, with archaeological evidence unearthed throughout the UAE indicating the presence of humans, albeit tenuously, as far back as 10,000 years, after the end of the Ice Age.

Ubaid pottery from Mesopotamia (modern-day Iraq), found in coastal excavations, dates back to 5000 BC, providing tangible evidence of the likelihood that Mesopotamian merchants traded their wares with local tribes, probably in return for copper (a valuable commodity that brought relative wealth to the area) mined throughout the Hajar Mountains.

Nomads living in the Arabian Peninsula herded goat, sheep and cattle inland during the winter months and fished in the Persian Gulf during the summer. Divers began to collect pearls from these waters at least as early as 4000 BC, while the resourceful invention of water irrigation channels – *falaj* (plural *aflaj*) – permitted agriculture to develop, even after the environment began to become more arid at around 1000 BC.

The cultivation of the date palm, one of the most crucial of oases flora, began around 2500 BC. Date palms were necessary for the survival of settled inhabitants: they are extremely nutritious and, after boiling, can last several months; livestock could eat crushed date pips; the leaves were used in weaving and binding; and the leaf stems and trunk were used in the construction of *'arish* (or *barasti*) homes. These somewhat fragile, semi-permanent huts were accompanied by more substantial mud-brick structures and watchtowers. Typically built at strategic, elevated vantage points throughout a tribe's territory, watchtowers stood

Al Fahidi Fort is Dubai's oldest structure and was built in the late 18th century.

19

Near the hamlet of Saham in Fujairah, a large rock contains a plethora of ancient rock carvings, including that of a man on a donkey, a man on a horse and a bull.

guard over their valuable date-palm groves, a necessary step as rivals coveted these fertile oases and the limited, yet crucial, resources they offered.

The tiny settlement of Dubai was first noted by the Roman chronicler Pliny, who described the Creek and the town of Dubai as Cynos in the first-century AD. Several groups migrated into the area from Yemen and central Arabia during the second-century AD, adapting themselves and their traditions to the new environment and surroundings they found.

ARAB CHRISTIANS AND THE ADVENT OF ISLAM

Christianity prevailed in numerous pockets around the Arabian Peninsula until the arrival of Islam in the seventh-century AD, evidenced by the discovery of a Christian Nestorian monastery on the island of Sir Bani Yas, in Abu Dhabi territory, by the Abu Dhabi Islands Archaeological Survey.

The Prophet Mohammad, persecuted in Mecca for his new beliefs, escaped north to Medina in September 622 AD. This was a significant event and was known as the Hegira (The Flight). This year also marked the beginning of the Islamic calendar.

The Prophet settled in Medina and his messengers began to spread the word of the new faith, until his death in 632 AD. A copy of an actual letter, allegedly written by the Prophet to Oman's rulers, is contained within Sohar Fort, written on a small rectangle of bleached parchment.

During the early Islamic period, from the 7th–14th centuries, many people settled along the Gulf coast, near a ready supply of fish and pearls. The Arabic language was introduced by the Islamic Umayyads, and there was a boom in maritime trade because of the area's central location between Europe and the Far East.

EUROPEAN CONQUERORS

In 1498, Portuguese Admiral and explorer, Vasco da Gama (1460–1524), established the first sea

Water irrigation channels – known as falaj *(plural* aflaj*) – channelled water to crops, enabling agriculture to develop in specific areas that would otherwise be dry.*

Dates were once a staple in the diet of the local inhabitants, and are extremely nutritious.

21

route from Europe to India with the help, many historians believe, of Ahmad ibn Majid, a well-known Arab seafarer. The Portuguese were quick to realise the strategic – and lucrative – importance of the Gulf and its role in the growing spice trade. In addition pearl-diving had been an occupational mainstay for coastal settlements for hundreds of years, with large pearling fleets sailing out to numerous pearling banks each summer to harvest the ocean and supply the world with the precious commodity, another attraction for the Portuguese, who recorded that: "Passing above this place Profam [Khor Fakkan] we come to another called Julfar [Ra's al-Khaimah], where dwell persons of great wealth, great navigators and wholesale dealers. Here is a very great fishery as well of seed pearls as of large pearls. . . ."

They fought to establish control of the peninsula's east-coast harbours, including the village of Khor Fakkan, now part of Sharjah, which was invaded by Alfonso de Albuquerque in 1507. The townspeople bravely tried to defend their town against a superior force, but they were overwhelmed. The young men were imprisoned and set to work in the galleys of the Portuguese ships, while the old men endured cruel mutilation by having their noses and ears cut off by their European conquerors. With victory across the east coast secured, for the next century-and-a-half at least, the Portuguese began constructing fortresses in various coastal settlements including Kalba, Khor Fakkan and Dibba to maintain control in the area from coastal and inland attack.

The small fishing settlement of 'Dibei' was referred to by Venetian jeweller, Gasparo Balbi, who visited the area in 1580 on a pearl-scouting trip.

The Portuguese dominated the area to such an extent that Arab coastal trade could not continue and local inhabitants were forced inland to The Liwa oases and Al Ain. The Portuguese, in turn, were expelled from the area by Omani forces in 1650.

The French, Dutch and British arrived in the 17th and 18th centuries. Great Britain's Delhi-based East India Company had set up trading contacts with the Persian Gulf as early as 1616, and one of its principal routes to India and back was the Red Sea and Persian Gulf, a route protected by Great Britain's naval fleet.

At the beginning of the 18th century, three tribal groups emerged to dominate south-eastern Arabia: the *bedu* of the Bani Yas confederation of tribes, who were based inland in The Liwa oases; the Al Bu Said tribe, who were based in Muscat, now the capital of the Sultanate of Oman; and the maritime Qawasim, who were based principally in Ra's al-Khaimah and controlled coastal ports on both sides of the Gulf, including Arabia's Sharjah and Fujairah, and Persia's Lingeh. The Qawasim fleet was believed to be so huge that it was a match for any of the European fleets, boasting some 900 ships, more than 60 of which carried 50

guns and 300 crewmen each.

Trade continued peacefully until the beginning of the 1800s. Francis Warden, Secretary to the Government of Bombay, which was responsible for the Persian Gulf, wrote, "From the period of their establishment in Oman until the year 1796, I have been unable to trace a single act of aggression, even on the part of the Joasmees (Qawasim), against the British flag." J S Buckingham, a British writer added that: "All (of the Qawasim), however, were so much more skilful, industrious and faithful in their engagements than the other tribes of the coast, that they were always preferred and constantly spoken of as the best people throughout the Gulf."

However, matters deteriorated as tribal and dynastic rivalry increased. French Emperor, Napoleon Bonaparte, having taken Egypt in 1798, intended to capture Muscat as part of his expansionist efforts, and use it as a springboard for an offensive against the British in India. As a result, the British allied themselves with the Al Bu Saids in Muscat, furnishing them with arms and ammunition to repel Napoleon.

The Qawasim viewed such an alliance as antagonistic. Resulting resentment, along with rich British and Indian cargoes of silks, teas and spices sailing past proved impossible to resist. The Qawasim were believed to be responsible for plundering passing British vessels and murdering their crews, leading the area to earn the name of the Pirate Coast. In one such infamous attack, the 5,000-strong crew of 55 Qawasim ships waylaid the *Minerva*, an East India Company vessel en route from Bombay to Bushire (in modern-day Iran), boarded the ship, cut her captain to pieces before marching every single crewman and passenger, bar one (who escaped and lived to tell the tale), to the

Above: Ortelius' map of the Middle East, dated 1573–1587, displayed at Sheikh Saeed House in Dubai.
Left: Pottery from the second-millennium BC was found in the Al Qusais area of Dubai.

gunwale upon which their heads were laid before their throats were cut.

The Qawasim were so effective that the Sultan of Muscat and Oman, Ahmed bin Said, along with his seven sons, launched a series of campaigns against them in 1805, 1809 and 1811. The pirates' activities were finally curtailed by Ahmed's grandson, Said the Great, who joined forces with the British Navy under the command of Sir William Grant Kier in 1819 to raze the Qawasim's fortresses in Ra's al-Khaimah and Lingeh, and burn their fleet.

The first signatory to Great Britain's general Treaty of Peace with the Gulf sheikhdoms on January 6, 1820, which guaranteed peace and British protection for 150 years, was Sultan bin Saqr, leader of the Qawasim and spokesman for Sharjah, Ajman and Umm al-Qaiwain, as well as Ra's al-Khaimah. A British political agent based himself in Sharjah to ensure adherence to the treaty.

In the book, *Western Arabia and the Red Sea*, a geographical handbook published by Great Britain's Naval Intelligence Division in 1946, what is now the UAE was then known as Trucial Oman. The book records this slice of history thus: "During the 19th century, Great Britain had imposed treaties on the rulers of Oman, Trucial Oman and Bahrein, requiring them to suppress piracy, gun-running and the slave trade, and to prevent the alienation of their territories."

THE BANI YAS

The activities of the Bani Yas confederation of tribes, the largest tribe in the UAE, were first recorded in 1633, when they were involved in a skirmish with warriors from Oman, between the coast and The Liwa oases deep inland, where the Bani Yas tribe were based.

In 1822, J N Guy, Lieutenant Commanding the HC *Marine*, provided the following description of Dubai: "Debai is the next town in succession to Sharga, from which it bears south-west by south a distance of 7.5 miles. It stands on the southern side of the entrance to a small creek. . . . The town is a simple assemblage of mud hovels, surrounded by a low mud wall in which are several breaches

and defended by three round towers, and a square castellated building, with a tower at one angle much dilapidated, and having only three or four guns mounted, which are old and rusty. The western tower, which stands on a small cliff over the creek, has also three or four guns, and is in a moderate repair. The inhabitants are in number from 1,000 to 1,200, and of the Beni Yass tribe. The district is under Sheikh Saeed, who maintains a body of 150 negroes as soldiers, or guards to the town. The inhabitants are supported by fishing, collecting sharks' fins, and particularly by the pearl fishery. Ninety boats are sent from hence in the season, and the yearly returns amount to between 20,000 and 30,000 dollars.

"There are two or three small date groves in which are contained the only fresh water wells in the place, at the back of the town; otherwise the country is uncommonly barren. From the tower, the creek was observed taking a winding course to the south-eastward for five or six miles, where it was lost in marsh. Its banks were studded with small brush wood, which, with rushes collected in the marsh, supply the inhabitants with fuel.

"Dates are procured from Bahrein, and a small quantity of rice from Muscat. . . . Mid way between Aboo Heyle and Debai stands a small village of about 20 huts, the inhabitants of which are fishermen, and a mile and a half to the south of Debai are two other small places, but neither of them are deserving of particular notice."

THE ARRIVAL OF THE MAKTOUMS

In 1833, some 800 of the Al Bu Falasah tribe of the Bani Yas confederation emigrated from Abu Dhabi to Dubai, after the recognised Ruler of Abu Dhabi since 1818, Tahnoon bin Shakhbut, was killed by his brothers, Khalifa and Sultan, in a coup. Lorimer (John Gordon Lorimer was an official in India's political service) reported the incident in his *History of the Persian Gulf*: "This violence on the part of Sheikh Khalifa (of Abu Dhabi) was highly prejudicial to his own interests, for it led to the secession from Abu Dhabi to Dibai, during the pearl fishery, of a large number of Bani Yas of the Al

Bu Falasah section. Dibai . . . seems to have been readily surrendered by the individual who then governed it . . . to the seceders; and they, in the following autumn, were joined there by the bulk of their relatives, returning from the pearl banks. The secession was permanent, almost the entire body of the Al Bu Falasah being to the present day domiciled in Dibai."

The Al Bu Falasah tribe was led by Maktoum bin Butti and Ubaid bin Said and, upon arrival in Dubai, the Maktoum family settled in Al Fahidi Fort, Dubai's oldest building located near the Creek.

The new sheikhdom struggled to defend itself against Abu Dhabi to the south and the Qawasim to the north, which each threatened to quash its fledgling independence. Maktoum bin Butti and Ubaid bin Said ruled jointly until bin Said died three years later in 1836, leaving Maktoum bin Butti to establish the Maktoum dynasty that still

rules Dubai today. He governed solo until he died in 1852, a year before the ratification of the Treaty of Peace in Perpetuity in 1853. This truce, to establish peace and abolish slavery, renamed the Pirate Coast as the Trucial Coast, and the contributing sheikhdoms became known as the Trucial States, a name that stuck until the formation of the United Arab Emirates in 1971.

When Maktoum bin Butti died, violence broke out among the family between the supporters of Maktoum's son, Hasher bin Maktoum, and Maktoum's brother, Saeed bin Butti. Saeed eventually wrested control and ruled Dubai until he died of smallpox in 1859. Seven years on from the death of his father, Hasher bin Maktoum was now old enough to take over the reins of leadership and, although the era was defined by violence, Hasher bin Maktoum ruled Dubai until his death in 1886.

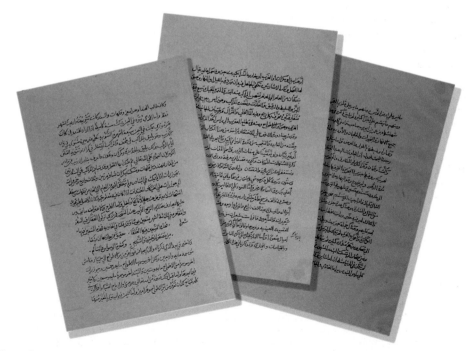

Pages from Ahmad ibn Majid's book Fawa'id, *written around 1490 AD and displayed at Sheikh Saeed House. The left-hand page is from the 'Sea Faring Seasons from the Coast of Arabia' chapter and the two right-hand pages are from the 'Description of World Coasts' chapter.*

Another power struggle ensued and Hasher's brother, Rashid bin Maktoum, forcibly took over. Hasher's sons, Maktoum and Majid, also challengers for the leadership, fled for fear of assassination.

Although they were never official British colonies, the Trucial States were protected by the British with representatives of Great Britain often called upon to mediate during times of tribal conflict. At the end of the 19th century (1892), Great Britain signed exclusive treaties with the rulers of the Trucial States, banning them from making deals with other countries without British consent. In return, the states would be further protected and British interests could be defended, a crucial move when the Ottoman Empire was crumbling and Tsarist Russia and Germany were beginning to focus their attentions on the Gulf.

In 1894, Rashid bin Maktoum died of suspected cholera, leaving the door open for Maktoum bin Hasher to return to Dubai to claim dominion, defying the claims of his much weaker uncle, Suhail, who was supported by his son, Butti; and Rashid bin Maktoum's sons: Said, Butti, Suhail, Mana, Hasher and Maktoum.

Plans were hatched to oust Maktoum bin Hasher, the new ruler, but before they could be enacted, Said bin Rashid and his brother, Butti, were arrested and incarcerated in Al Fahidi Fort for a short time, before being exiled to Sharjah, where they remained for more than a decade.

PERSIA'S LOSS IS DUBAI'S GAIN

Dubai began to acquire its fame as an important commercial port during the rule of Maktoum bin Hasher. There was a flourishing blackmarket arms trade, and some 120 rifles were smuggled through Sharjah and Dubai in September 1902, with more

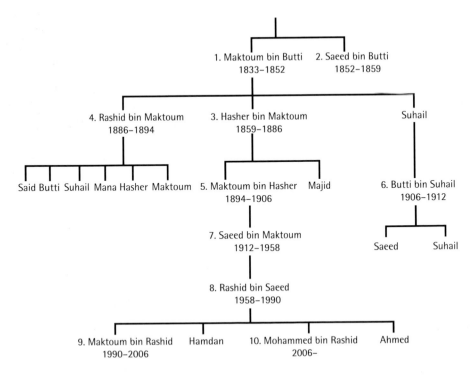

The Maktoum family tree (males only), from 1833 until the present.

than 200 a month later, according to Lorimer's *History of the Persian Gulf*. As such, gunrunners were actively pursued by Britain's Royal Navy.

In 1887, the Persians, desperate for tax revenue, had forcibly retaken control of Lingeh Port from the Qawasim incumbents and, in 1902, they transferred the running of Lingeh Port to Belgium, whose officials attempted to apply the same methods used in Europe, including high import and export customs duties, to collect revenue. This was a mistake.

Capitalising on this, Maktoum bin Hasher offered full tax exemptions to traders from abroad, resulting in entrepôt trade from India deviating from the Persian coast, especially Lingeh, straight to liberal Dubai. As a result, many Persians from the area of Bastak migrated to Dubai, and the town became a distribution hub for, not only maritime trade, but trade from the interior as well, especially from the verdant Buraimi Oases near Al Ain.

Building upon this success, Maktoum bin Hasher convinced the British India Steam Navigation Company to make Dubai its main port, and the company's mail steamers, known locally as the Ups and the Downers (*Maaley* and *Sanaan*), began arriving in Dubai every fortnight, en route to and from Bombay from 1903. In five years, Dubai's port was thriving, with 50 retail outlets in Bur Dubai and some 350 in Deira. Along with increased trade came an influx of immigrants from Iran, India and Balochistan (a region of Pakistan), keen to prosper from Dubai's relaxed atmosphere.

In 1906 and, after a relatively long rule of 12 years, Maktoum bin Hasher died. His son Saeed was too young to assume power, so the leadership passed to Maktoum's cousin, the elderly Butti bin Suhail.

Lorimer's *Gazetteer of the Persian Gulf* reports began in 1903 (and were completed in 1915), when

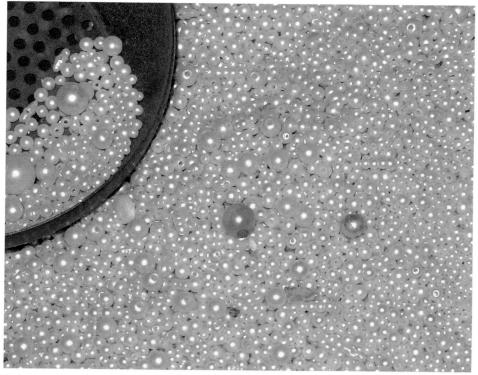

Divers began to collect pearls from local waters as early as 4000 BC.

he accompanied Lord Curzon, the Viceroy of India, on his tour around the Persian Gulf, which took in Dubai. One of his reports in 1908, displayed at Sheikh Saeed House in Dubai, describes the town: "Dibai is situated between the sheikhdoms of Sharjah on the north and Abu Dhabi on the south, meeting Abu Dhabi at Khor Ghanadhah, which runs inland for many miles and divides the principalities one from the other. Jabal Ali, the only hill on this coast, is in Dibai territory; it is 220 feet high, flat topped and lies 19 miles south-west of Dibai town and four miles inland, being separated from the sea by a strip of low desert. . . .

"Besides Dibai Town and the village of Hajarain [Hatta], the only permanently inhabited place in the principality is Jumaira, a coastal village about three miles south-west of Dibai Town; it is consistent of 45 date-branch huts and is inhabited by Bani Yas, Manasir and mixed tribes who are all fishermen and own among them five camels, 60 donkeys, 45 cattle and 200 sheep and goats.

"The sheikh maintains about 100 retainers armed with Martini rifles, and about 1,500 of his ordinary subjects are reported to be similarly armed. There are no customs at Dibai Town, but the revenues of the principality are said to amount to $51,400 a year, largely derived from the pearl fisheries. Dibai stands on both sides of a creek, with a shallow and difficult entrance, which extends for some miles beyond the town in a south-easterly direction; there is a small quay for vessels able to go inside. Shandaghah is the residence of the Sheikh of the Dubai Principality and contains some 250 houses all occupied by Arabs; Indians are not allowed to establish themselves here. Dibai proper contains about 200 houses and 50 shops, also the principal mosque and some ruins said to be those of a fort; the Indians are all collected in this quarter.

"Ferry boats ply between Dairah and Dibai proper, and on Fridays the crossing is free to inhabitants of Dairah who go to worship in the Jami mosque. There is good water at Dibai in wells from five to 30-feet deep. The town was once walled, but the wall is now in ruins. On the landward side,

A small oasis deep in The Liwa oases.

however, are a number of towers of defence.

"Date trees number about 4,000, but the yield is scanty; the only other cultivation is a little lucerne. Dibai Town is reckoned to possess 1,650 camels, 45 horses, 380 donkeys, 430 cattle and 960 goats. About 335 pearl boats, 50 fishing boats and 20 seagoing vessels, the last being chiefly *sambuks* and *badans*, belong to the place, and 10 to 12 boats are built annually.

"The trade of Dibai is considerable and is rapidly expanding, chiefly in consequence of the enlightened policy of the late Sheikh Maktum bin Hashar, and the stringency of the Imperial Persian Customs on the opposite coast; Dibai is now in the process of supplanting Lingeh as the chief entrepôt of the foreign trade of Trucial Oman. . . .

"The only exports of local origin are pearls, mother-of-pearl shells and dried fish. The imports are dates from Basrah, Minab and Batinah; also rice, wheat, piece-goods, spices, metals, coir rope and timber, chiefly from India. The town contains some 400 shops and 200 warehouses. A portion of the imports are destined for the interior, particularly for the Baraimi Oasis. Of the local merchants, 23 are Hindus and seven are Khojas under British protection".

In December 1910, several heavily armed sailors from HMS *Hyacinth* landed in Shindagha in the early hours of the morning in pursuit of arms dealers they believed had docked a few hours previously. Many local inhabitants, under the impression they were under attack from the British, began firing on the sailors and a gun battle ensued throughout Dubai's narrow streets, which lasted for several hours. Four sailors were killed and nine injured. The British retreated and demanded 50,000 rupees in compensation (Indian rupees were the Gulf's currency at this time), permission to install telegraph facilities and a post office, and the surrender of some 400 rifles.

However, Great Britain was not pleased with the fracas and sent a letter from the British Empire in India, on January 3, 1911, reprimanding HMS *Hyacinth*'s Commander and the British Political Resident. It said: "The government of India is not satisfied with the situation which has arisen in Dubai. From your telegram, they gather that the search of houses took place without the sheikh being present. If this were the case the actions of the commander were likely to provoke reprisals and were hardly prudent. Some of the conditions imposed on the sheikh they consider onerous."

They weren't the only ones upset by this action by the British. Butti bin Suhail was furious and penned a letter to the region's most senior British diplomat who was based in Lingeh: "You know full well my attitude of reverence and respect to the British government, also, by the Grace of God, I am not one of those who oppresses others. We experienced such things at the hands of His Majesty's boat's crew who were there, as we have never experienced before. At 5.00am the captain of the man-o'-war landed with his troop of about 100 sailors. The moment they arrived they began slaughtering and killing my men . . . it was afterwards that I found out that 37 of my men were killed."

After only six years in charge, Butti bin Suhail died in 1912, and the leadership passed to Saeed bin Maktoum, Butti's cousin and the son of former Ruler, Maktoum bin Hasher.

In 1912, Al Ahmadiyyah School, for boys only, was founded by philanthropic pearl merchant Ahmad bin Dalmuk, with lessons consisting of Arabic, maths, Islam and the pearling trade. The first schools for girls in Dubai, Al Khansaa in the home of Sheikha Shamsa bint Sultan (Rashid bin Saeed's mother-in-law) in Deira and Khawla bint Al Azwar School in Bur Dubai, opened more than 45 years later in 1958. Lessons included classical Arabic, geography, history and science.

When it became obvious that Persian customs duties would not be lifted in the 1920s, Saeed bin Maktoum offered the Persians an area along the Creek in which to settle and call their own, located near Dubai's main souk to the east of Al Fahidi Fort. The new quarter became known as Bastakiya and, today, with its renovated *barjeels* (windtowers) and narrow *sikkas* (streets), it stands as a proud reminder of the harsh existence before the discovery of oil.

By the 1930s, immigrants accounted for

Above: It was spacious inside the khaimah *hut as shown in this recreation at Dubai Museum.*
Right: The outside of a khaimah *hut with its windtower, recreated at Dubai Museum.*

nearly 25 per cent of Dubai's population of 20,000. The burgeoning town was believed to possess the largest souks in the Gulf region, a state of affairs that proved crucial when, in the 1930s, the Japanese cultured pearl and world depression devastated the Gulf, resulting in high unemployment, civil unrest and poverty to such an extent that people were reported to be dying of starvation.

Many of the local population were forced to lay off their retained staff as the economic crash gripped the region and they saw their prosperity decline. They only had their slave labour to fall back on, although the British were keen to stamp out slave trading in the Persian Gulf, and manumission, the act of freeing a slave, was actively encouraged.

By the late 1930s, some 50 Dubai slaves had applied for their freedom. This number increased in 1937 and 1938 and, when Great Britain threatened to enforce manumission across the board, Saeed bin Maktoum came under heavy criticism from local merchants and several cousins for not standing up to them.

IN ANTICIPATION OF OIL

The first oil concession was granted by Saeed bin Maktoum to the Iraq Oil Company on May 22, 1937, although no oil was discovered and the concession eventually lapsed in 1961.

Two months later, on July 23, 1937, Saeed bin Maktoum and the British Government signed a civil air agreement allowing Imperial Airways' (the forerunner to British Airways) Empire Flying Boats to land en route from Southampton to Karachi. The base was rented for just 440 rupees a month (Dhs35 at today's rate), which included the salaries of the airstrip's security guards, and a fee of five rupees (later 10 rupees) was levied for each landing. By 1938, four flying boats landed per week. By 1944, this had increased to eight a week.

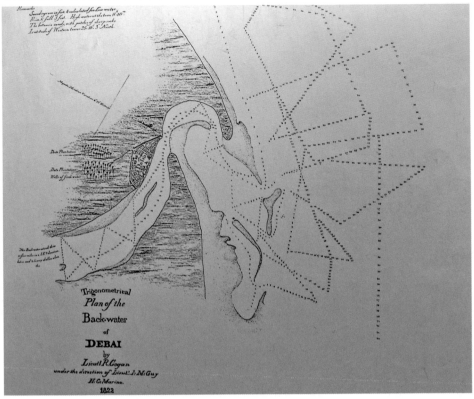

Above: An 1822 map of 'Debai' by Lieutenant R Cogan under the direction of Lieutenant J M Guy, on public display in Sheikh Saeed House in Dubai.
Right: Maktoum bin Hasher's pocket watch. He ruled Dubai from 1894–1906.

THE SHEIKH'S WIFE

In this patriarchal society, women were rarely in the public eye; their husbands kept them in the background and all but immediate family were forbidden to glimpse their features. Which makes the public role of Saeed bin Maktoum's wife, Hessa bint Al Murr, even more remarkable; certainly a liberal flame in these dark, misogynistic times. Those seeking a meeting with Saeed bin Maktoum often had to pass through Hessa first, although she protected her modesty by use of a heavy curtain. She had the authority to change policy and provided advice to the government. She also moulded her son and future Ruler, Rashid bin Saeed, into a determined, ambitious fighter.

THE MAJLIS

Tribal spats and power struggles divided the Trucial States' ruling families, including those of Abu Dhabi, Sharjah and Dubai. In fact, few rulers endured the ambitions and plans for accession from friends and family, with patricide and fratricide common practices round the Persian Gulf at that time.

The crash of pearling, one of Dubai's lifelines, had hit many local merchants extremely hard, including Mohammed bin Ahmad bin Dalmuk (whose father had founded the first school in 1912), and the Ruler's cousins, Mana bin Rashid, Hashar bin Rashid, Saeed bin Butti and Suhail bin Butti. They called for reforms to customs, privileges and conditions, and set about gathering support for themselves and their cause.

Saeed bin Maktoum's gentle nature – he was described by Captain T Hickinbotham, the Acting Political Agent in Bahrain, as "one of the pleasantest persons on the coast with whom to have dealings, as he always behaves like a gentleman" – was perhaps viewed as weakness because, as far as his cousins et al were concerned, the 1930s offered them a golden opportunity to overthrow him.

Indeed, in 1934, Saeed's wife, Hessa bint Al Murr, along with his son, Rashid, had asked for help from the Royal Navy to arbitrate in the increasingly worrying situation.

News filtering through of a similar movement in Kuwait, where the Ruler was forced to share power with an elected council, offered much encouragement to Saeed's opponents.

However all the cousins' suggestions for change were dismissed automatically, as Saeed bin Maktoum feared they had an alternative agenda and were trying to depose him.

Matters came to a head in October 1938, with Saeed bin Maktoum's supporters encamped in Dubai and his cousins and their supporters in Deira. Saeed bin Maktoum's grip on power eventually weakened and, after discussions, he was urged to sign an agreement on October 20, which set in motion the inauguration of a 15-member consultative council, otherwise known as The Majlis, with expenditure one of the central issues. In the agreement, Saeed bin Maktoum was granted an allowance of one-eighth of Dubai's total revenue, and any monies generated by Dubai had to be used for the benefit of Dubai and sanctioned by The Majlis.

During the six months The Majlis survived, it tackled practical reforms to improve the lives of Dubai's citizens. However, Saeed bin Maktoum grew increasingly resentful at his treatment by The Majlis and, after initially attending the meetings, he stopped going altogether and did all he could to obstruct Majlis decisions. When The Majlis decided, at the beginning of March 1939, to amend the Ruler's income from a percentage of Dubai's profits to just 10,000 rupees, he'd had enough.

Responding to the threat, Rashid bin Saeed seized the initiative during his wedding to Latifa bint Hamdan Al Nahyan on March 29, 1939.

There are several views about what happened next. Some commentators say that several *bedu*, attending the wedding, dispersed opponents; others say that Rashid bin Saeed masterminded a stealthy operation, captured his opponents and seized the Deira Customs House among others; while others say that, with the support of several loyal tribal sheikhs, Rashid opened fire against his opponents, killing three of his cousins: Said bin Rashid, Butti bin Rashid and Hasher bin Rashid.

Soon afterwards, another cousin, Mana bin Rashid, set up a Municipal Council on the northern side of the Creek in Deira.

On the eve of World War II in 1939, Abu Dhabi's ruler, Shakhbut bin Sultan Al Nahyan, granted the first oil concession within his territory. But, with no properly defined borders between Abu Dhabi and Dubai, disagreement was inevitable between the two rulers: Shakhbut and Saeed. However, the onset of World War II in September 1939 not only suspended hostilities along with oil-prospecting operations, but resulted in a standstill in trade, upon which Dubai relied.

Although the sheikhdoms and surrounding area were not directly involved in the war, their strategic location and oil potential meant that allied troops were never far away, particularly British troops tasked with keeping an eye on things. In addition, it was important for the British to maintain their link to India by defending the airstrip in Sharjah, which opened in 1932 and was a crucial refuelling point.

The situation with Saeed bin Maktoum's

cousins had not gone away either. On January 26, 1940, as World War II got under way, Rashid bin Saeed and his retinue were attacked by some 50 armed men while they were camped three miles from Deira. A gun battle ensued for an hour or so, and there were several deaths on both sides before the raiders retreated.

The battle resumed a week later at Dubai's northern end (now Al Mamzar Park), between Rashid bin Saeed and his supporters against some 200 opponents who had encamped at Al Khan, Sharjah's most southerly end and separated from Dubai by Al Khan Creek. The battle lasted for several months with cannon and guns, although when civil or military aircraft flew over the area, the parties called a ceasefire.

Edward Henderson, an oil-company representative, diplomat and resident in the Gulf during this time, wrote in his autobiography, *Arabian Destiny*: "Imperial Airways, the forerunner to BOAC, would still refuel their flying-boats on Dubai Creek and send the passengers over to the

fort in Sharjah for lunch. During this operation the war was suspended by mutual agreement between the belligerents, and passengers would pass through the 'lines' without, in most cases, realising anything unusual was afoot, since the air crews, who knew about it, had no wish to alarm them by explaining it."

When World War II ended in 1945, a resumption in oil prospecting and the accompanying border dispute between Abu Dhabi and Dubai, which was now in effect ruled by Rashid bin Saeed, was rekindled once more, ultimately leading to war. Lasting three years between 1945 and 1948, the war was typified by traditional raids and counter-raids, with valuable property, such as camels, the main targets rather than human life. However, the killing of some 50 members of the Manasir tribe brought the belligerents to their senses, and they sued for peace.

The British stepped in and, drawing upon their research into the tribal use of the area (by sending a diplomat into the wilderness, astride a camel, to

Spices from the Indian subcontinent have been traded in Dubai for centuries.

talk with village elders, tribal chiefs and *bedu*, to establish to whom they owed allegiance), dictated where the border should be set between Abu Dhabi and Dubai, to Dubai's advantage.

THE FIRST BANK

Keen to improve its commercial pedigree to complement developing trade and the economy, the first bank on the Trucial Coast, the Imperial Bank of Iran (later The British Bank of the Middle East and now HSBC Bank Middle East), was called in to set up in Dubai in 1946.

The bank introduced documentary credit banking procedures to replace the traditional spot cash basis of trade operations. The activities of The British Bank of the Middle East were not restricted to simple commercial banking; it contributed to many additional worthwhile activities, including the administration of finance for the Customs Department and raising much-needed funds for Dubai's early development.

HYGIENE AND HOSPITALS

Before proper medical facilities, inhabitants of the area suffered with numerous diseases, including tuberculosis, syphilis and leprosy among others. According to *Western Arabia and the Red Sea*, a leper colony existed near Dubai. "Next to Dibai, south-west of Sharja, is a little village which is the leper asylum for the entire Pirate Coast; once a week the lepers may enter the towns and beg. . . . Recent increased immigration from Baluchistan has brought in many new cases."

Dubai's settlers lived in huts made from palm fronds, or in houses constructed from local gypsum and coralstone, with roofs built from *chandel*, or mangrove, poles. There was no sewage system so, other than a few pits dug in private dwellings, many local inhabitants used the Creek and the open air as their lavatory. As a result, fish caught from the Creek were used as bait, and never used for human consumption. However, Ronald Codrai, who lived in Dubai from 1948 until 1955, noted

Silks were also traded, a precious cargo that arrived in Dubai from the Far East.

that the town was "remarkably free of those sorts of unpleasant smells," because of the cleaning properties of the sea, tides, sand, sun and fish.

The first hospital in Dubai and indeed, the Trucial States, was the Al Maktoum Hospital. Constructed with the help of the British, Dr Donald McCaully, a former British India military doctor and now Senior Medical Officer for the Trucial States, began practising at the hospital in 1949.

It complemented Dubai's first health centre, a small clinic manned by a general practitioner, which had opened in 1943 in the Al Ras area of Dubai. The new hospital included both an outpatients' department and segregated inpatients' departments, which each had six beds. By 1973, the number of beds had increased to 157 in each department.

GOLD SMUGGLING

Dubai diversified into the smuggling of gold into India at a time when it was illegal to import gold into that country. As much as today's Government of Dubai tries to deny its gold-smuggling

The renovated Bastikiya area, on the banks of the Creek. Pictured are barjeels, *or windtowers.*

credentials, there is much anecdotal evidence of this activity making a huge impact on the town, especially during the 1950s and 1960s, when gold smuggling reached its peak. In the 2005 book, *Telling Tales, An Oral History of Dubai*, which recounts the life stories of several now elderly UAE nationals, many can remember the gold-smuggling days only too well; they tell of how the gold was smuggled into India, the risks they took and the danger this illicit activity involved. Edward Henderson also recounts stories of gold smuggling in *Arabian Destiny*.

As a result of what it saw as gold-smuggling activities, India took the dramatic step of withdrawing its rupees (the region's currency at that time) from the Gulf by the end of 1966, in an attempt to halt the illegal activity.

The Gold Souk in Deira, now brimming with tourists, is a lasting legacy of these Indian smuggling rackets, or legitimate re-export markets, whichever you choose to believe.

LAW AND ORDER

The discovery of oil in the early 1950s brought with it the need for increased security measures. The Trucial Oman Levies was formed in 1951 (later renamed as the Trucial Oman Scouts) under the command of a British officer, Major Mike Hankin-Turvin, to maintain law and order and guide oil-company exploration teams into the country's interior. Based in Sharjah and reporting directly to the British Political Agent in the Gulf, the unit consisted of 200 men, mostly recruited from Abu Dhabi's *bedu* population.

In 1951, Britain created the Trucial States Council (the forerunner of today's UAE Supreme Council), chaired by the British Political Agent and made up of the rulers of the seven Trucial State sheikhdoms, who would meet twice a year to discuss policy.

On June 1, 1956, a police force was founded in Naif Fort. Jack Briggs became Commandant of Dubai Police in 1965 and, during the decade he served in that role, he moulded the force into something resembling a modern police service.

CHANGE OF LEADERSHIP

During the last 17 years of Saeed bin Maktoum's life, his son, Rashid, effectively ruled the country, officially succeeding his father on September 10, 1958. Rashid successfully quashed Mana bin Rashid's Municipal Council, which had become known as The Deira Movement and, defeated, members fled to Sharjah and Abu Dhabi.

Rashid then set about merging both the Deira and Dubai side of the Creek, and allied himself with oil-rich Qatar by marrying his daughter off to its Ruler, Ahmad bin Ali Al Thani. Dubai's coffers filled with Qatari wealth and Rashid was able to begin to modernise his tiny, cash-starved sheikhdom, gathering together Dubai's merchant families to rally to his cause, including the Al Ghurairs, Al Futtaims, Al Naboodahs, Galadaris and the Lootahs among others, the next generation of whom still hold court in Dubai to this day.

Referred to as the 'Father of Dubai', Rashid bin Saeed set about updating the town's medical and electricity services, and improved the facilities for water, which, until that time, was still manually hauled from wells.

Improvements brought an increase in the population along with the introduction of a modernised police force, which was funded by both the Dubai and British governments.

Dubai Creek, on which the town's prosperity was based, was gradually becoming clogged with silt, and the resulting sandbanks were in danger of completely cutting off the Creek from the Persian Gulf. Eventually, boats were only able to enter and exit at high tide. Matters at Sharjah Creek had been even worse, so much so that, by the early 1950s, trading dhows that used to unload their goods at Sharjah began using Dubai instead. This change in fortune had prompted Britain's Political Representative to move his base of operations from Sharjah to Dubai in 1953.

One of the most crucial decisions Rashid bin Saeed made after becoming Ruler was to dredge the Creek in 1959. It was an expensive procedure, but one that was vital for Dubai to retain its position as a regional trading centre. The gamble

paid off, so much so that, nearly 40 years later in 1995, Dubai accounted for 70 per cent of the UAE's total trade. Other sheikhdoms had baulked at the cost, but with a loan of £200,000 from a local bank and £400,000 from the Government of Kuwait, dredging began.

Also that year, Dubai opened its first hotel, the Airlines Hotel and, soon after, launched new water and electricity companies. Rashid bin Saeed also established what is now Dubai International Airport, sited some four kilometres from the centre of the town on a wide strip of *sabkha* (salt flats). The runway measured 1,800 metres and came with a small terminal building and accompanying fire station. Large enough to accommodate DC3 (Dakota) aircraft, the airport began operations from 7.00am to 1.00pm each day with Herons and Dakotas in September 1960, which was later increased to 18 hours a day the following year, and 24-hour operations a few years later.

In 1960, there was not a single tarmac road in Dubai. The population consisted of three small communities: Deira, on the northern side of the Creek, Bur Dubai on the other side of the Creek, and Shindagha at the mouth of the Creek. During the 1960s, the Land Department, headed by the Ruler's son, Maktoum bin Rashid, was established, along with Dubai Municipality in the town's Souk Al Murshid area. The first Municipality budget was 2,500 rupees (Dhs200 at today's rate) and its first car was a second-hand jeep from the British RAF base in Sharjah.

In 1961, a Ruler's Decree was issued from Dubai Municipality and the first municipal council was created to provide the whole emirate with essential services. From this starting point, which was characterised by a serious shortage in construction material and the availability of a very modest budget, development began slowly.

Construction of a network of roads, initially designed by Rashid bin Saeed, started at one kilometre of road per month. Finance was obtained from Rashid's son-in-law, the Emir of Qatar, for the construction of Maktoum Bridge, which linked Bur Dubai with Deira and opened in May 1963. The National Bank of Dubai also opened in 1963. The

The Gold Souk is a lasting legacy of the Indian gold re-export, or smuggling, trade.

Clocktower Roundabout was unveiled in the 1960s (and has been a landmark ever since), along with Garhoud Bridge and an underwater tunnel that connected Shindagha to Deira.

Work began on the airport's asphalt runway in 1963. The new runway ran parallel to the existing strip for an increased length of more than 2,800 metres, so that much larger aircraft could be accommodated. It was inaugurated in May 1965 with the arrival of jets from Middle East Airlines and Comets from Kuwait Airways. Further improvements were made to the airport including the construction of new hangars, baggage-handling facilities, terminal buildings and a control tower. By 1969, the airport was accepting flights from nine airlines that flew to 20 destinations.

The Trucial States Development Council was set up by the British in 1965, to speed up development. Revenue from oil, which had recently been discovered in Abu Dhabi's offshore territory in 1958, began to pour into that emirate's coffers, but the Ruler of Abu Dhabi, Shakhbut bin Sultan

Al Nahyan, who did not trust banks, or foreigners for that matter, was unable to cope with his new wealth. As a result, and with British help, Zayed bin Sultan Al Nahyan ousted his brother in a bloodless coup in August 1966.

The town's first automated telephone exchange opened in 1966 and, more importantly that year, oil was discovered in Dubai's offshore Fateh field (*fateh* means 'breakthrough' in Arabic), located some 90 kilometres west of the town.

In 1967, an outbreak of smallpox prompted Rashid bin Saeed to implement a large vaccination programme and upgrade his medical facilities with the opening of Rashid Hospital. When, in 1970, both Dubai and Ra's al-Khaimah succumbed to a severe outbreak of malaria, facilities were in place to vaccinate some 60,000 residents.

THE OIL BOOM COMETH

In 1969, Dubai began to export its oil, with the first tanker taking delivery of 180,000 barrels of

The Creek, Dubai's raison d'etre. *Pictured in the distance is the Emirate of Sharjah.*

crude oil on September 22. Before shipment, the oil was stored offshore in huge sub-sea *khazzans,* the Arabic word for storage. Each *khazzan* was 70 metres tall and 90 metres in diameter. Originally constructed by The Chicago Iron & Steel Company, they were located in an area 20 kilometres south-west of the centre of Dubai, on an isolated stretch of beach that became known as Chicago Beach. A new hotel, the Chicago Beach Hotel, was soon built on the same stretch of beach. Demolished in 1997, it was replaced by the Jumeirah Beach Hotel.

Exports continued, generating revenues that brought new opportunities for Dubai's development. With the onset of oil production, the Creek's access inlet was widened and a new harbour was constructed to collect customs duties.

The number of ships entering Dubai in the late 1960s reached a total of 4,000 every year. Work began in 1969 on a deep-water port made up of four wharves at a total cost of £9 million. Later, it was decided to expand the project to include 15 wharves at a total coast of £23 million. Port

Rashid was officially opened on October 5, 1972 and, in 1978, further expansion of the port was undertaken to accommodate yet more wharves.

THE WITHDRAWAL OF THE BRITISH

In 1968, the British Government led by Labour Prime Minister, Harold Wilson, announced its intention to withdraw from areas east of Suez by the end of 1971, exactly 151 years after the general Treaty of Peace signed by the British and the Gulf sheikhdoms in 1820, guaranteeing peace and British protection for 150 years.

This cost-cutting exercise stunned many of the ruling Trucial States sheikhs along with the rulers of Bahrain and Qatar, who began considering their options. Few of them appreciated the formidable task of establishing an effective government and defensive infrastructure that, until that time, had been operated with assistance from the British. Concerned, the rulers bandied together and the Ruler of Bahrain, Isa bin Salman Al Khalifa, mooted the idea of an alliance between all the Gulf States.

Zayed bin Sultan and Rashid bin Saeed met at the village of Al Samha, along the border of Abu Dhabi and Dubai, on February 18, 1968, and agreed to partially unite their sheikhdoms in terms of foreign affairs, defence, security, immigration and social services. In addition, they sent out invitations to the rulers of adjacent sheikhdoms: Sharjah, Fujairah, Ra's al-Khaimah, Ajman and Umm al-Qaiwain, as well as to the rulers of Bahrain and Qatar, to join them in creating an alliance that would enjoy a far louder voice across the entire Middle East region.

All nine rulers met for two days during the following week to put aside their tribal squabbles and thrash out a plan. At the conclusion of the meeting, although an agreement was signed by all nine rulers setting in motion the creation of a new alliance, the rulers of some of the smaller sheikhdoms began to grow nervous about losing control over their territories.

More meetings were held over the next couple of years to try and assuage fears and to reach accord over constitutional issues, including the location of a new capital city on the border between Abu Dhabi and Dubai, with Zayed bin Sultan emphasising during one meeting in October 1968: "Abu Dhabi's oil and all its resources and potentialities are at the service of all the emirates."

Meanwhile, Dubai continued developing quickly, with the first traffic lights making an appearance on Dubai's streets in 1969 and, in 1970, the Department of Health and Medical Services was established, tasked with modernising health-care services. This was followed with the construction of Dubai Hospital in 1983, Al Wasl Hospital in 1986 and, in 2006, the beginnings of construction of Dubai Healthcare City, the world's first health-care free zone.

The rulers met for pre-Federation talks again on July 10, 1971 to discuss a unified police force, exchange controls and the licensing of alcohol for

Above: The Clocktower Roundabout, one of Dubai's oldest structures built in the 1960s.
Right: Oil was discovered in Abu Dhabi's offshore territory in 1958.

The last moments of the Chicago Beach Hotel, built in the 1970s and demolished in 1997. The Jumeirah Beach Hotel's Conference Centre can be seen on the right, while the Burj Al Arab takes shape behind.

The wave-shaped Jumeirah Beach Hotel replaced the Chicago Beach Hotel.

non-Muslims. At the end of the meeting, Saqr bin Mohammed, the Ruler of Ra's al-Khaimah, held off signing the provisional constitution.

Negotiations collapsed when Bahrain and Qatar chose independence in August and September 1971 respectively. However, the Trucial States remained determined to forge ahead with creating an alliance. The British formally departed the Trucial Coast on December 1, 1971 and, the following day, the six emirates of Abu Dhabi, Dubai, Sharjah, Ajman, Umm al-Qaiwain and Fujairah announced the formation of a new state, the United Arab Emirates. Abu Dhabi's Zayed bin Sultan was elected as President, with Dubai's Rashid bin Saeed elected as Vice-President.

Four days later, the UAE became a member of the Arab League and, in that same month, it joined the United Nations.

In January 1972, the Ruler of Sharjah, Khalid bin Mohammed, was killed by the ex-Ruler of Sharjah, Saqr bin Sultan, who had been deposed in 1965 in a British-backed coup. Reports of the account can be read in *From Trucial States to*

United Arab Emirates and on Mohammed bin Rashid's website, which states: "A group of 18 rebels, headed by Sheikh Saqr bin Sultan himself, shot their way into the Ruler's palace. Shooting and hand grenade explosions could be heard clearly by some residents in Dubai and Sheikh Rashid scrambled Union Defence Force troops from Dubai city to join those from Sharjah at the scene. The force from Dubai was headed by Sheikh Mohammed bin Rashid, who was present throughout the crisis".

The report adds that the murder was a culmination of several previous attempts, including the secretion of explosives under Khalid's *majlis* chair in 1970 and the attack by a gunman on the Deputy Ruler, Saqr bin Mohammed, in 1971. Sultan bin Mohammed Al Qasimi (now Dr Sultan) took over from his brother, and has ruled Sharjah, off and on, ever since.

In February 1972, Ra's al-Khaimah agreed to join the alliance by becoming the seventh and final emirate in the UAE. The formation of the UAE precipitated an influx of immigrants from India,

Villagers living in the Hajar Mountains are always inquisitive of strangers.

Persia and other Arab states throughout the new country and boosted the population from 180,000 to 560,000.

GROWING PAINS

The path to uniting the emirates was far from smooth. Although each emirate retained a certain amount of autonomy, the President, Zayed bin Sultan, was eager to centralise power, much to Dubai's opposition.

When Zayed bin Sultan proposed a federal budget and the unification of each emirate's armed forces in 1979, Rashid bin Saeed refused. The ensuing stalemate became so frustrating to the President that he threatened to resign. It was only when a member of the Kuwaiti royal family intervened that the looming crisis was diffused.

That same year, Rashid bin Saeed suffered a stroke and, as a result, he began to shift some of his responsibilities over to three of his four sons, Maktoum, Hamdan and Mohammed.

In 1980, security concerns brought into focus by the Iran/Iraq war resulted in the formation of the Arab Gulf Cooperation Council (AGCC) in 1981 with membership consisting of Bahrain, Kuwait, Oman, Qatar, Saudi Arabia and the UAE.

Another stroke in 1981 incapacitated Rashid bin Saeed to such an extent that, although he officially remained Ruler of Dubai until his death in 1990, his sons took over the reins of power. He was wheelchair-bound, blind and was almost unable to speak.

The modern incarnation of Dubai International Airport was inaugurated by Rashid bin Saeed in May 1971, which enabled the airport to accommodate Jumbo jets and Concorde and, in 1985, Emirates airline began operations with two leased aircraft operating to three destinations: Karachi, Bombay and Delhi. The airline has since become one of the fastest-growing airlines in the world and has greatly contributed to the image of Dubai as a commercial and tourist destination on the international stage.

The number of airport passengers increased from 4.3 million in 1988 to 9.7 million a decade

UAE nationals practice the traditional stick dance, or ayyalah, *in front of onlookers.*

later, an increase of 125 per cent. By 2004, numbers had increased to 21.7 million and, official estimates are that by 2010, Dubai International Airport will cater to some 60-million passengers. The Sheikh Rashid Terminal was opened in 2000 and, by 2004, the airport was able to accommodate 107 airlines, which connected to more than 160 destinations across the world. Expansion continues with the construction of the new Emirates-dedicated Concourse 2 and 3 and Terminal 3. Scheduled for completion in 2007, the airport will have the capacity for nearly 70-million passengers a year. Another airport, Dubai World Central International Airport, located south of the city in Jebel Ali will, when complete in 2008, be the largest airport in the world at an immense 140-square kilometres (twice the size of Hong Kong island), which will be able to handle more than 12-million tonnes of cargo and cater for 120-million passengers per year; more than the entire populations of the UK (60 million), Australia (20.7 million), Canada (32.2 million) and Switzerland (7.5 million) combined.

A NEW BROOM

Rashid bin Saeed died on October 7, 1990, and he was succeeded by his first son, Maktoum

UAE women dressed traditionally in a thin veil (gishwa) left, and face mask (burqa), right.

bin Rashid, who ruled in a largely ceremonial role. The de-facto ruler was, in fact, Maktoum's younger brother, Mohammed bin Rashid, who was appointed Crown Prince in 1995 to drive the emirate forward into the 21st century and transform Dubai into a regional business, tourism, IT and aviation hub.

Mohammed bin Rashid was a man born to achieve and is fortunate to be surrounded by good advisors and assets estimated to be in excess of £7 billion (according to online encyclopaedia, Wikipedia). Not content with the mundane, he wants to see ambitious plans to place Dubai on the world stage come to fruition . . . and quickly.

Four years after taking on the mantle of Crown Prince, the iconic Burj Al Arab opened for business in 1999. He has instigated many trail-blazing initiatives, including the world's largest artificial islands, Dubai Waterfront & Arabian Canal, the Dubai International Financial Centre and numerous residential property developments.

In 2001, Mohammed bin Rashid issued instructions to clamp down on government corruption and 14 officials were arrested, according to the *Gulf News*. Following the 9/11 terrorist attacks, recommendations by the Paris-based Financial Action Task Force (FATF) to fight money laundering were implemented and, in August 2002, the US praised Gulf countries for their efforts, especially the UAE, in the pursuit of fighting terrorist financing.

Following the death of Maktoum bin Rashid

in January 2006, Dubai is now officially ruled by Mohammed bin Rashid. Mohammed, also the UAE's Minister of Defence, now assumes the additional roles of the Prime Minister and Vice-President. Known as the 'CEO of Dubai plc', he is the architect of modern Dubai and is accountable to no one within the realms of his very own sheikhdom. He, like Dubai's rulers before him, is the absolute ruler of a hereditary, tribal dictatorship.

But who will succeed him? Although it's still early days, Mohammed bin Rashid has not named a successor. He has two living brothers, the elder Hamdan and the younger Ahmed; and a sister, Mariam. He also has 16 children; seven sons and nine daughters (again according to online encyclopaedia, Wikipedia), including Rashid,

Hamdan, Maktoum, Saeed, Ahmad and Majid. His eldest son, Rashid, appeared as if he was being groomed for leadership, but, until the latter part of 2006, had been absent from public life for more than a year. No official reason was ever given. Sons two and three, Hamdan and Maktoum, took his place and were regularly photographed by the media accompanying their father during his many official engagements.

Although it's uncertain as to who will be the next Ruler of Dubai, perhaps Mohammed bin Rashid will break with tradition and demonstrate his vision and wisdom to the world by nominating one of his daughters as the next Ruler of Dubai, such as UAE ladies karate champion, Maitha, or his acclaimed artist niece, Hessa bint Maktoum. Only time will tell.

WORKING LIFE

If you're coming to live in Dubai, you, your husband, wife or partner are most probably coming to work. With so much competition for jobs at home, you have many more opportunities to do what you want in Dubai than elsewhere, especially if you have a university degree and know the right people, because there's such a shortage of quality individuals in the workforce.

However, if you're used to Western, staff-friendly working conditions, employment in Dubai may come as something of a shock.

According to figures published in *Gulf News* in April 2006, there are some 2,738,000 expatriates working for 246,420 companies in the UAE.

With so much cheap labour from Asia and Eastern Europe, certain jobs are, in effect, closed to Westerners, including many 'trade' occupations, such as carpenters and plumbers; petrol-pump attendants, shop assistants, construction workers and waiters and waitresses.

> Top tip: When you come to Dubai to work, don't expect the same working conditions you may be used to in the West. For many, they work too many hours for too little pay for too little quality of life.

There are also several crucial points with which you need to be aware. Once you sign a contract (which may be fixed-term or open), the company for which you work has to sponsor you. As part of the process of acquiring sponsorship and obtaining your residence visa, you must provide a blood sample, which is tested for communicable

Construction workers queue for the bus at the end of their long day at Dubai Marina.

49

diseases. Many government organisations (including schools) will also require a chest X-ray. If you show any indications of disease, you'll be deported straight away.

Your life is, for the most part, dictated by the company for which you work, whether you need to rent a villa or apartment, want a bank loan to purchase a car, want to subscribe to some mobile-phone services or obtain a liquor licence; all well and good if you work for a respectable company; but what happens if you don't?

Top tip: Be warned that if the company you work for fails to carry out its legal obligations with regards to visas, labour cards, sponsorship etc, you're likely to be the one detained by the police.

CASE STUDY – ABSCONDER

Through no fault of your own, it's rather too easy to fall foul of the law with regards to visas and working arrangements in Dubai.

I was working for a Dubai Media City company, Company A. It sponsored me and, as such, I enjoyed legal status with a residence visa and labour card. Unfortunately, the company was taken over by its competitor, Company B. I asked my new boss about my sponsorship and whether his company was now legally required to transfer my sponsorship to it, but he was quite indifferent to the matter, saying that, as both companies came under the umbrella of Dubai Media City, there was no problem and there was no need to change things.

I thought, as an employer, he should know what the procedures were, so I carried on, blissfully unaware, for the next six months or so before I was made redundant in a staff shake-up.

I didn't sit on my laurels, but managed to get another job quite quickly with Company C. I asked for and received a No Objection Certificate from Company B and, as I had to leave the country to cancel my sponsorship with Company A/B, and then return on a visit visa so that Company C could begin the procedure for sponsoring me, I went home to the UK for a holiday.

A couple of weeks later, I returned to Dubai and arrived at the airport in the darkness of a very early Friday morning (Friday is the UAE equivalent of a Western Sunday). When I got to Customs, the official tapped my name into her computer, frowned and said, "*Mushkula, mushkula,*" which means 'problem' in Arabic.

I think I was arrested, although I wasn't informed I was under arrest, but I was aware I wasn't free to go. In any case, I was taken to a back room and told to sit down on a chair alongside several other worried-looking people. My passport was handed to a stern-looking policeman in green uniform, who sat on the other side of a desk completing paperwork. When he looked up I caught his eye and asked what the problem was. He looked at my passport and tapped my name into his computer.

Unfortunately, he didn't speak much English and all he could say was "*Mushkula, mushkula.*"

I had no idea what I'd done wrong, or how I was going to get myself out of this mess. After sitting around for about 20 minutes, wracking my brains and watching people coming and going, the policeman looked at me and said in broken English: "You have friend with passport, get you out, or you in jail until Saturday." This freaked me out! It was around 1.30am by this time and I wondered who would be up at this time of night. I phoned a UAE national friend of mine who was still awake and willing to come to the airport with her passport. In this way, she'd lodge her passport with the police and, in effect, take responsibility for me and bail me out. I was made to feel like a criminal.

My friend found out from the policeman that I'd been 'detained' because the system showed that I had absconded from the company I worked for, which clearly didn't make any sense.

It transpired that my sponsorship should have been transferred to Company B and not as my indifferent boss had told me. As it was, I had remained under Company A's sponsorship, a company that now no longer existed and, when the trade licence for Company A expired, I was logged as an absconder for some reason, which still didn't seem to make any sense as how could I abscond

Traditional Arabian occupations, such as gargour (top) and net making (above), are seldom carried out by UAE nationals these days, but by those from the Asian subcontinent who, in this case, live on-site too.

from something that didn't now exist?

Anyway, my friend got me out and we were told to report to the airport police again on Saturday to sort everything out. It was a worrying time. I was made to feel guilty for something that was my employer's responsibility and over which I had no control.

But not every company is like this. There are some very efficient, very aware companies in Dubai that not only genuinely believe their staff are their most important asset, but also believe that a work/life balance is crucial for productivity, and employee motivation and morale. If you're lucky enough to work for a company that adopts these enlightened principles, grab it tightly and never let go.

Up until 2004, many employers would even keep an employee's passport as part of the conditions of employment, denying employees their freedom of movement, a policy that contravened a 2002 directive issued by the Ministry of the Interior, which stated: "A passport is a personal document that proves the identity of the holder, and the laws stipulate the bearer must keep their passport and present it to the authorities upon their request."

Yet although companies cannot now legally force their employees to hand over their passports, far too many companies, including the government if local press reports are to be believed, still flout the law.

CASE STUDY – EXCELLENT BOSSES

I'm British and have worked for a multinational company in Dubai for more than 10 years. When my mum was first diagnosed with cancer, I was offered immediate leave for a few days to let the news sink in. I declined because I thought it was best to keep busy.

I took various trips in the year to see my mum in the UK, all within the bounds of my annual leave. When it came to the last few months, I flew home in June/July to be with her, using some of my annual leave. I then returned to Dubai for a couple of weeks before I was called back to the UK again

because she'd taken a turn for the worse and wasn't expected to live beyond a fortnight. I had prepared my bosses for the news that I might get called away; I was assuming I'd be taking unpaid leave, their only request was that I had full handover procedure notes.

We'd had a meeting earlier to decide who was going to cover for me while I wasn't around. Everyone knew what they had to do well in advance in case I got the call; my work colleagues were all fabulous. I flew back to the UK on 2 August and my mum eventually died on 28 August. I had to then spend another two weeks in the UK sorting out her house etc. I called work every few days to tell them what was going on; my boss called me about once a week, each time beginning the conversation with, "I'm not calling because I want you back at work, I want to know if you are ok." I was worried about work and told him my thoughts.

The General Manager then called me and told me to take as much time as I needed, the company would write off the leave I had taken and I would not have anything deducted from my salary. I was told not to worry, everything would be fine for when I got back. This really did help me an awful lot. I already had the stress of watching my mother die; my company relieved me of any extra burden and enabled me to deal with my home situation without having to think about work.

Six weeks later, when I eventually returned to Dubai, of course I'd blown my annual leave by over six weeks. However, my boss sat me down, took out my annual leave card, he wrote some notes on it to the effect that I had taken additional leave, free of charge, and signed it off.

The next thing that happened surprised me – he credited me a week's leave to take between September and Christmas; my company's theory was that I'd been under a tremendous amount of stress and that I should take a week out for myself, because I'd not really had a holiday in 18 months. So I went to Sri Lanka for four days, played some golf and came back refreshed.

I'm not sure I would have held up so well if I'd had that additional pressure of having to return to work and leave my mother at home . . . I probably would have had no option but to resign. From that point of view, the company was great and made me feel valued as an employee. My boss and General Manager are both British and have been through similar experiences – I think these factors played a very important role in how I was treated.

Initially, I was worried I would feel indebted to them, and I did to start with. Every time my boss asked me to go the extra mile I felt like I had no choice; although he never made any comments. I guess I was a bit paranoid. That didn't last very long though.

The company is just the name, it's the people in the company that made this happen for me; it's not a corporate policy. I could have been with my company and had different bosses who stuck to the rules of allowing me to take one week's compassionate leave with a loss of five weeks' salary. People are human beings not companies and just because you work for a multinational, you must not make the mistake of thinking this would apply to you. I now have a new boss; he may not have done that for me. But personally, I love working for the company . . . I always have.

THE LABOUR LAW

The UAE Law No 8 of 1980, as amended by Law No 12 of 1986 (the Labour Law), governs employer/

employee relations, such as hours of work, leave, termination rights, medical benefits and repatriation. This law is meant to protect employees – and it does to a certain degree – although the employee has little recourse if it's defied. Why foreign domestic and agricultural workers are not protected by the UAE Labour Law is unknown, and leads, in some cases, to serious exploitation of this sector of the workforce. However, according to the *Gulf News* in November 2006, Sheikh Mohammed ordered the Naturalisation and Residency Department to put into practice special contracts between servants and housemaids, and their employers, that would grant them their full rights and limit their working hours.

In an attempt at updating the 20-year-old law, the government posted a new draft Labour Law on the Internet at the beginning of 2007, and invited the public to comment. As a result, Human Rights Watch compiled a 15-page report that outlined the draft law's deficiencies. See http://hrw. org/backgrounder/mena/uae0307/ for full details.

The maximum working hours for the private sector are officially eight per day, or 48 hours per six-day week (with nine hours for those in retail, hotels and restaurants). However, 10-hour days over a five-day week are common, with no overtime paid and, in some cases, no time off in lieu of overtime worked either. The majority of the

It's not unusual for job adverts to stipulate the nationality and gender of candidates.

Above: Checking text messages in the area of Deira while waiting for a job.
Left: These Asian fishermen are using whatever they can at their disposal to make a living.

private sector employs expatriates (a mere 804 UAE nationals worked in the private sector in mid-2006, according to the *Gulf News*), with working hours ranging from 8.30am to 6.30pm, or split into shifts, such as 8.00am to 1.00pm and 4.00pm to 9.00pm.

Some 88 per cent of government, public-sector employees are UAE nationals. Working hours differ markedly from those in the private sector, with many government departments open from only 7.30am to 2.30pm. Within the public sector, working conditions differ noticeably between UAE nationals and expatriates too. A report in the *Gulf News*, for example, stated that expatriate employees of one government department were promised a 15 per cent pay increase in April 2005; they were still waiting for it in April 2006; while UAE nationals were given a 25 per cent pay rise at the same time and received it immediately.

During Ramadan, companies are obliged to reduce their working hours to six, particularly if they have Muslim staff, but not all do. There are some 10 public holidays a year, but not all companies allow their staff the days off, or compensation for

working them. Annual leave is usually 30 calendar, or 22 working days a year. Public-sector employees enjoy far more holidays than those in the private sector; according to the *Gulf News*, the average working days per year for the public sector are 180 and, for the private sector, 275.

The official weekend for the public sector was changed in September 2006 from Thursday/Friday to Friday/Saturday. While many private-sector companies already operated a Friday/Saturday weekend to remain as close as possible to the Western working week, the government is studying whether it should apply this ruling across the board to all private-sector companies because, according to the Federal Labour Law, only Friday is a day off.

It's likely that many businesses will continue to operate a six or five-and-a-half-day working week, failing to realise the business benefits of a five-day working week on the productivity and morale of their staff. Following the decision, the *Gulf News* conducted a poll of residents who were unanimous in their call for all private-sector employees to enjoy a two-day weekend.

One of the entrances to Dubai Media City.

A FAIR DEAL IN THE WORK PLACE?

There seems to be little concept of fairness when working in Dubai; the colour of your passport tends to decide the level of job for which you can apply. It's the norm, for example, for job adverts to stipulate the nationality and gender of candidates (eg US/UK-educated female).

Salaries also differ according to nationality; for example, a hotel worker from the Philippines told the *Gulf News* that, as a waitress with two years' experience, she earned just Dhs900 a month. Yet a Romanian colleague, doing the same job, earned Dhs1,300 a month.

Unfortunately, this issue is well known by anyone who's spent more than five minutes working in the UAE.

Recognising the problem, Dubai Municipality announced, in 2006, that it had embarked on the Labour Characteristics Survey. A consultant with the Municipality's Statistics Centre told the *Gulf News*: "We want to see if there is discrimination among professionals based on their nationalities, and see the level of wages according to profession and educational background."

In December 2006, the *Gulf News* reported findings from the Statistics Centre which revealed that a massive 77 per cent of Dubai employees are dissatisfied with their jobs. Citing wages as a major factor for their unhappiness, the poll was

And working hours that chain you to your desk for at least 10 hours a day give you little time or the energy required to enjoy or appreciate the quality of this new life you've moved several thousand miles to experience.

You may be used to working flexitime, or part time. However, you'll find very few opportunities to do so in Dubai. Full-time working is the rigid norm. So much so, that many working parents don't get to see their sons or daughters, except during their one or two-day weekend.

Of course, with the attitude of "Well if you don't like it . . . leave" discussed previously, companies simply cannot evolve, as people do, indeed, take them at their word and leave. This lack of evolution has resulted in outdated working practices being the norm for many in Dubai.

Even managers who lure you with the promise they work along Western lines may have been in the UAE too long to recognise what these standards are any more and, as they have little incentive to change, they can treat staff as they like. The resulting clash for many 21st-century employees, working in these conditions, which are also heavily stacked in the employers' favour, becomes untenable very quickly.

JOB HOPPING

Once you have a job, it used to be quite difficult to change if you were unhappy with your salary or working conditions. Up until August 2005, the Six-Month Ban was regularly used by employers to threaten disgruntled staff who rocked the boat. Application of this ban meant that, not only did you lose your job, but you were forced to leave the country and not return for six months.

However, to change jobs now, you must obtain a No Objection Certificate (NOC) from your employer. If they won't issue you with one, for example, if you want to work for a competitor, you must wait six months before getting another work visa. However, you're still able to stay in the country on a visit visa. If you're from the West, the law is simple to circumnavigate, as you're allowed far more flexibility with your passport than other

conducted with 8,130 families. In addition, the average time it took people to get to work was 46 minutes each way.

FLEXIBILITY IN THE WORK PLACE?

Many people come to Dubai seeking a better quality of life, shorter working hours, a great tax-free salary and a work/life balance. While this is true in many respects, certainly when it comes to entertainment and leisure, several perceptions differ markedly from reality. Many people work exceptionally long hours, for seven days a week in some cases, with a working week that would leave many from home balking at the strain.

nationals, such as those from India, Pakistan, Eastern Europe and South Africa.

> Top tip: Explain the NOC situation to your new boss and he/she will postpone the paperwork for six months. You'll work on a visit visa, which is technically illegal, although standard practice. A visit visa lasts two months, so you need to make three visa runs, ie you leave the country and return the same day (Oman and Qatar are popular destinations), thereby obtaining a new stamp in your passport as you re-enter the country.

Why the government does not encourage a dynamic, fair job market, where employees are free to vote with their feet by penalising bad employers, without fear of reprisals, is anyone's guess. It's such an obvious thing to want to do. Not only would backward companies be encouraged to adopt modern best practices, such as family friendly flexitime and work/life balance principles to retain staff, but by doing so, they would increase their employees' morale, productivity and loyalty into the bargain. Not only that, if employees feel they make a real difference, they're likely to stay longer.

If Dubai is serious about playing with the big boys on the international stage, it simply has no choice but to improve working conditions and provide a level playing field for employees. In this way, it will not only continue to attract quality people, but will be able to retain them over the long term too.

CASE STUDY – EMPLOYEE BEWARE

Beware of companies who're at pains to tell you they're Western managed and run and all this implies about a fair working environment and conditions. You may find it somewhat different in reality. The alarm bells first sounded when my boss specifically told me not to tell anyone my salary, and the longer I worked for him, the more I came to the conclusion that he was devoid of any moral fibre or integrity. The *Oxford English Dictionary*

summed him up perfectly: he was a shyster; an unscrupulous or disreputable person in business.

Investment in people did not exist. Equality did not exist. Training and development did not exist. Bullying was rife, with unethical processes and procedures the norm. And I could do nothing about it. After seven months, the company had still not undertaken its legal obligation to sponsor me and issue me with a residence visa and labour card, even though I used to ask for this on an almost weekly basis. I didn't have a contract either. In this case, you're working on goodwill alone, hoping that, if you work hard, eventually you'll be rewarded and treated fairly; no more, no less.

However, the company treated its staff like children who were all patronised on a daily basis. Technical equipment was not sufficient to expedite given tasks and when we raised the issue, the boss told us he didn't have enough money to purchase all the tools to do the job; and yet all of us were still expected to 'pull the rabbit from the hat' every single day.

We were expected to work during Muslim holidays, including a full nine to 10-hour day during Ramadan, which is illegal. During this holy month, one employee had an accident, which involved a short stay in hospital and some temporary disablement. The employee returned to work while disabled, fearing that, if she didn't get back to work as soon as she could she'd be sacked. She was sacked for no reason a week or so later anyway.

Another employee, 11 months into their contract, was sacked, again for no apparent reason. Even though they were extremely pleasant, efficient and hard working, conflict with the boss may have been the reason, although a cynic (or perhaps a realist) may take into account the length of service with respect to the issuing of a plane ticket, which all companies must provide to their employees after 12 months' service.

Another employee, new to Dubai and without a UAE driving licence, was ordered by the boss to attend a meeting some distance away and to take one of the company's cars for the purpose, even though the boss was aware the employee had no driving licence and was therefore not insured to

These construction workers, toiling on one of numerous high-rise buildings at Jumeirah Beach Residence, have hard hats, and safety harnesses to protect them from falling.

drive the vehicle. Although the employee protested, he worried he would be sacked if he didn't acquiesce. Unused to the roads and driving on the right, the employee had an accident en route to his meeting. Upon reporting back to the office, the employee was told he must take out a bank loan to pay for the damage to the car, because the repairs obviously wouldn't be covered by insurance, although it was also impossible for the employee to take out a loan as he had no residence visa and the company was too small to be on any bank's 'approved companies list'.

This toxic, blame-culture company had employed and sacked more than 25 people during the previous 18 months. Its appalling track record was directly linked to the high turnover with regards to the development and treatment of staff for the long haul. Alienation was company policy to those not favoured on a personal level by the boss, whether they could expedite tasks or not. There was no set standard and no equality, which caused huge resentment. Yet, if we complained or made too much fuss, we all feared we would simply be sacked, which is easy to do in a system weighted heavily in favour of the employer, while employees had no rights and no recourse whatsoever.

EMIRATISATION

Getting UAE nationals into the workforce is known as emiratisation, and its aim is to replace many occupations currently occupied by expatriates with indigenous people. All government departments are headed by UAE nationals, with the majority of government ministers hailing from the UAE's ruling families: the Al Nahyans of Abu Dhabi, the Al Maktoums of Dubai and the Al Qasimis of Sharjah.

For example, the UAE President is Sheikh

There's nothing to stop these construction workers, working at a site next to The Greens (above), and those erecting an advertisement along Sheikh Zayed Road (left), from falling.
Following spread: Construction at Dubai International Airport's new terminal and concourses.

Khalifa bin Zayed Al Nahyan; the Crown Prince of Abu Dhabi and Chief of Staff of the Armed Forces is his brother, Sheikh Mohammed bin Zayed Al Nahyan. Two more brothers are Deputy Prime Ministers of the UAE: Sheikh Sultan bin Zayed Al Nahyan and Sheikh Hamdan bin Zayed Al Nahyan. The UAE's Vice-President, Prime Minister and Minister of Defence is the Ruler of Dubai, Sheikh Mohammed bin Rashid Al Maktoum, whose brother, Sheikh Hamdan bin Rashid Al Maktoum, is the Minister of Finance and Industry. There are two women in the cabinet: the Minister of Economy, Sheikha Lubna bint Khalid Al Qasimi and Mariam Mohammed Khalfan Al Roumi, the Minister of Social Affairs.

Although the government has made it law to employ a certain percentage of UAE nationals in the private sector (currently two per cent in companies with more than 50 employees, and five per cent in the banking and insurance sectors) many companies have simply ignored the ruling as the law has been hard to enforce.

The government also believes some jobs or job grades are beneath its nationals, including those encompassing manual labour, working in retail (unless it's as a manager) or driving a taxi. Suitable jobs include upper and middle management, accounting, finance, IT and engineering. Unfortunately, this policy guarantees the UAE is likely to remain fully dependent on expatriates to

61

maintain its core infrastructure for many years to come and, as such, UAE nationals will probably remain a minority in their own country.

The Human Resources Development and Employment Authority's (Tanmia) figures show that only 9.3 per cent of the entire work force are UAE nationals. However, despite government efforts and those of Tanmia to enforce quotas, and train and assist graduates to find work, the number of jobless UAE nationals continues to grow; some 33,000 at the last count.

One sector already emiratised is that of PROs, or public-relations officers. Once the bastion of Asian workers until December 2005, PROs are tasked with expediting company transactions with government departments, including the issue of labour permits and residence visas. The government decreed that the 2,700 Dubai companies with more than 100 employees had to employ a UAE national PRO, and those that didn't would not have their transactions processed. However, by April 2006, only 1,600 nationals had been employed as PROs and, according to a Ministry of Labour official, many companies were circumventing the law by employing a UAE national for display purposes only; the real work was still being carried out by the existing Asian PRO who, if asked, was 'assisting' or 'training' the UAE national.

Following on from this, the government announced plans in mid-2006 to roll out emiratisation to other occupations, including those of secretaries and human resources (HR) staff, a move that worried the business community. Non-national secretaries could no longer renew their visas, although since the new ruling, companies can now apply for an exemption.

The plans to emiratise HR, whose practitioners usually come with many years of training and experience under their belts, caused much concern. However, the government ruled that HR managers must be replaced by UAE nationals within 18 months. Companies working in free zones, however, are exempt from this new emiratisation policy.

Emiratisation is likely to remain a difficult process for many years to come, as not only do the private sector remain reticent to its adoption, but UAE nationals don't help their government's cause either. A top police official told the *Gulf News* in January 2006 that he blamed parents for providing their children with a too-easy lifestyle when only 16 of the 455 UAE national candidates, put forward for jobs in the police service by Tanmia, accepted a job, when more than 80 per cent was expected. Despite concerted efforts to reach them, 274 candidates had switched off their phones, did not answer or had provided incorrect numbers, and 65 failed to finish their appointment procedures.

CAMEL JOCKEYS

In May 2005, the UAE penned an agreement with UNICEF to rehabilitate and repatriate child camel jockeys and, as a result, some 2,000 boys have been sent home to Bangladesh, Eritrea, Pakistan, Mauritania and Sudan.

Since then, the UAE has earmarked £4.6 million for former child camel jockeys employed in the country, which will cover outstanding salaries, compensation for losing their income and education. Camels are now ridden by remote-controlled robots instead of, traditionally, adult men, which is one custom the country seems happy to lose. Developed by UAE national engineers, each robot costs around Dhs7,300.

MAIDS TO ORDER

Having a maid or houseboy in Dubai is not a luxury but an absolute necessity, especially for those who work long hours. Numbering around the 300,000 mark, these 'servants' hail mostly from Asian countries and, unfortunately, languish at the bottom of Dubai's social pecking order alongside construction workers.

Recruited by agencies, they're sent out to sponsors or domestic-cleaning companies. Although many maids have fun, enjoy employment and a better quality of life in Dubai than in their home countries, some are lured to the city under false pretences; for example, they're told they will be arranging flowers in a top hotel, only to find the reality somewhat different.

The UAE has outlawed the use of children as camel jockeys, replacing them with robots that each cost around Dhs7,300. The top picture was taken in 1998 and the bottom, in 2006.

Above: Construction workers at Dubai Marina wait for the bus to take them back to camp.
Left: Dubai International Financial Centre under construction.

Many find themselves sharing accommodation with several others, with evening curfews and harsh punishments if they rebel. And, after signing up with a company or sponsor for a couple of years (and relinquishing their passports) it's virtually impossible for them to leave the country without permission.

Others, according to the local press, are mistreated. In the past few years, there have been stories of maids dying while trying to escape by jumping from balconies; and maids, having escaped, showing evidence of physical and mental abuse, to name but a few.

A housemaid's woes are added to when she seeks comfort in another's arms. Local press reports tell of maids receiving lashes for becoming

pregnant out of wedlock, followed by deportation; and other 'servants' receive six-month jail sentences for having 'illicit' affairs with each other.

The Indonesian Government actually banned its nationals from working as housemaids in the UAE, according to the *Gulf News* in January 2005, "following some cases of abuse". The government in Dubai has, however, acknowledged the problem and is seeking ways to make life a little better for its maids and houseboys.

CONSTRUCTION WORKERS

Local press reports about construction workers, and many of the companies for which they work, strike

Above: Poor living conditions have been the cause of much anger among workers.
Left: Construction at Dubai Marina. Traffic congestion, along Sheikh Zayed Road, can be seen in the distance.

There are some 500,000 construction workers in the UAE, mostly hailing from the Indian subcontinent.

as disturbing a note as that of maids if they're to be believed. This is often exacerbated by the failure of construction companies concerned to respond to questions posed by the media when incidents occur.

There are some 500,000 construction workers in the UAE, each earning between Dhs400 to Dhs1,500 a month, depending on their skills. According to official figures, 20 construction workers died in 2003, 34 died in 2004 and 39 died in 2005, an upward trend likely to persist if some developers continue to care little about the welfare of their workers.

Hailing mostly from the Indian subcontinent, many construction workers are treated little better than animals, herded into labour camps with hundreds of others to live in cramped, squalid conditions. Things get so desperate that, according to local newspaper reports, fights break out over access to such basic human needs as cold drinking water. In addition, some camps get so full that

workers are forced to live outside, braving temperatures that, during a summer's night, hover above 30°C. Some construction workers are not even paid, relying on handouts from charities or good Samaritans to merely exist.

In the past, if they rocked the boat, construction workers were dealt with severely; there were even stories of workers being locked up in their compound by their sponsor for complaining about non-payment of salaries.

Even though strikes are illegal in the UAE, some workers are driven to such depths of despair they are forced to protest. In 2005, there were a total of 31 protests and, by mid-2006, there had already been 20 strikes staged, 12 for non-payment of salaries stated the *Gulf News*.

The plight of construction workers finally reached the world's media in March 2006, when 2,500 construction workers on the Burj Dubai and airport-expansion projects went on strike. The

Workers taking a well-earned break find anywhere to sleep, as long as it's out of the midday sun.

protest revolved round non-payment of overtime, poor transport arrangements and shoddy living conditions in the workers' camps.

Strikes and increasingly violent protests continue however, as workers see their peaceful demonstrations fall on deaf ears and little improvement in their lives, leaving them with no choice but to 'up the ante' each time. Dubai has seen riots, destruction of company property and company directors taken hostage. According to *7DAYS*, the Indian Consulate blacklisted 27 construction companies in Dubai in 2006, in an attempt to halt their nationals being exploited.

The government has taken its time in addressing the issues. This is, perhaps, not surprising: after all, there are few precedents to which it can refer; it's used to its expatriates doing what they're told without question and disgruntled expats simply leaving Dubai if they don't like it. So instead of looking at how it can improve by

addressing the underlying causes of these violent protests, ie poor living and working conditions, it simply deports dissenters instead, paving the way for a fresh batch of workers; workers who are likely to do exactly the same as their predecessors, or worse, once they've reached their tolerance threshold, if the status quo is not improved.

However, there does appear to be light at the end of the tunnel for construction workers. Dubai Police's Human Rights Care and Social Services Department has set up a hotline to cater for complaints of non-payment of salaries and, in November 2006, Sheikh Mohammed ordered the Ministry of Labour to introduce compulsory health insurance for all construction workers.

In addition, Dubai Municipality established a committee to monitor and report on the health and living conditions of site workers.

The Ministry of Labour has also asked the government for Dhs120 million to pay for additional inspectors to enforce the Labour Law and tackle rogue companies. From having just 25 inspectors in July 2005, it's expected some 2,000 will eventually be recruited, charged with monitoring construction workers' living and working conditions.

Group 4 Securicor is leading the way with the construction of a new kind of residential complex for its employees called David's Village (named after Group 4's regional Vice-President David Hudson), where some 2,000 of its guards can enjoy a gym, library, medical facilities and other benefits. In addition, Dubai Investment Park, in partnership with Seven Seas Shipchandlers, is creating cricket and football pitches for its construction workers.

At present, there are no trade unions in Dubai and strikes remain illegal. However, in order to boost free-trade negotiations with the US, the UAE announced in March 2006 that workers would be able to form trade unions with the power of collective bargaining by the end of the year for the construction, fishing and agriculture industries (although at the time of going to press in 2007, any law had yet to be passed, and seems unlikely ever to be passed if a report by Human Rights Watch is to be believed; see http://hrw.org/english/docs/2007/03/25/uae15547.htm for more details).

OUTSIDE IN THE HEAT

There are currently no laws stating the maximum temperature employees can work in, although a ministerial order, dating back to 1982, states that employers should "eliminate excessive humidity, and excessive high or low temperatures. . . ."

It's unknown just how many construction workers die each year of heat-related illness or injury, although some deaths are reported in the local press, the last one as recent as July 2007.

As a result, some construction-company bosses see no reason why their employees shouldn't work outside in the summer desert heat, sometimes for more than 12 hours a day, six days a week.

A journalist attempted to work outside for the whole day alongside a gang of construction workers as part of a report highlighting their plight. He

lasted just a few hours before being admitted to hospital with heatstroke and dehydration.

A subsequent public outcry during the summer of 2005 prompted the government to introduce a four-hour break from working outside in searing temperatures between 12.30–4.30pm during the hottest months of July and August.

However, in 2006 (and now 2007), this break was reduced by an hour-and-a-half to between 12.30–3.00pm, a compromise that pleased no one; some UAE contractors feared a loss of too much money, with no consideration for the human cost, while the labourers complained that even 2005's four-hour break was too short. One construction worker put it succinctly to 7DAYS: "Before they make the decision, we would like them to come and work with us in the blazing sun."

Around a third of all construction companies in Dubai and the Northern Emirates were caught flouting the 2006 midday break law. With an increased number of inspectors now tasked with photographing and reporting violations, it's hoped the figures for 2007 will be much improved.

And according to one Dubai-based meteorologist, the summer heat is set to rise further in the foreseeable future, possibly a result of the 'heat island' effect caused by the UAE's continuous infrastructural development.

CONSTRUCTION CRISIS

According to a report by the Emirates Evening Post in April 2006, Asian workers had become so disillusioned with Dubai that, coupled with the improving economies in their home nations, many were returning home, leaving Dubai's construction industry in crisis. In fact, some recruitment agencies have stopped sending workers to Dubai completely because of the low pay, unsatisfactory working conditions, exorbitant charges and lengthy visa processes.

With an increasingly disgruntled expatriate workforce and some 33,000 unemployed UAE nationals, one sector that's crying out to be emiratised is the construction industry. In this way, UAE nationals could really contribute in a hands-

The studios of Al Arabiya in the MBC Building, Dubai Media City.

on role to the development of their own country, instead of relying on others to do it for them.

FREE ZONES

Free zones were introduced into the UAE in 1985 to cater to certain business sectors, which has allowed businessmen and women to set up their own companies and enjoy 100-per-cent ownership. Free zones in Dubai include the Jebel Ali Free Zone, one of the world's largest industrial centres; Dubai Airport Free Zone, Dubai Internet City and Dubai Media City.

As part of Sheikh Mohammed's policy of globalisation, he began to court 'knowledge-economy companies' and 'knowledge professionals' both from the world of IT and media. In order to do so successfully, he realised he had to provide an attractive infrastructure and environment in which they could work.

In 1999, he decreed that Dubai Internet City (DIC) be built within 365 days along Sheikh Zayed Road near to the Hard Rock Café. Wooed with huge incentives, such as 100-per-cent ownership (ie companies did not need to have a UAE national partner to trade) and tax-free-zone status, the US$250 million DIC did, indeed, open within the year, although it was still a work in progress. Heavy hitters, including Microsoft, Oracle, HP, Dell and Siemens, moved in to their state-of-the-art, fully serviced offices, creating a wealth of resources and expertise on tap, and all in one place.

To date, there are more than 800 companies and some 5,500 personnel working out of DIC. Complementing DIC is the adjacent Dubai Media City (DMC), which was opened in 2001. Also with tax-free-zone status and a state-of-the-art infrastructure, it promised to offer companies and individuals the 'freedom to create'. It currently houses some 1,000 companies, including CNN, Reuters and BBC World; and several freelance professionals. According to its website, the freedom of expression for media is guaranteed in DMC, along with 100-per-cent foreign ownership;

DMC currently houses some 1,000 companies, including CNN, Reuters, BBC World, Al Arabiya and MBC.

and, rather than being tax-free, there's a guaranteed 50-year exemption from personal income and corporate taxes. However, no one has dared challenge this freedom of expression guarantee because, even as recent as 2006, there were calls from the UAE's top judiciary to stop the detention of journalists.

Setting up a business in one of Dubai's many free zones is becoming increasingly expensive. The cost of trade licences and rising rents are forcing many small-to-medium-sized organisations to seek alternative accommodation, away from Dubai's exorbitantly priced free zones to those in other emirates. Figures from research conducted by the *Gulf News* are compelling: it costs around Dhs22,000 to set up a small business at Ra's al-Khaimah Free Zone and operate for a year; around Dhs25,000 in Sharjah's SAIF Zone; yet between Dhs85,000–100,000 for a similar operation in Dubai.

SMALL BUSINESSES

To set up your own business in Dubai, you need a trade licence, which is issued by the Dubai Economic Department. You should also register your company with the Dubai Chamber of Commerce and Industry (DCCI). Business categories for expatriates include a joint-venture company, a shared partnership company and a limited-liability company, the most popular option for small businesses employing between two and 50 members of staff.

If you want to set up a limited-liability company, you need a minimum capital of Dhs300,000, along with a local sponsor, who will own 51 per cent of your company, while under no obligation to contribute anything. However, during 2006, the WTO attempted to push the government to relinquish the requirement for a UAE partner.

If you start a small business, it's quite likely the overriding climate of fear permeating Dubai will lead many members of your staff to tell you what they think you want to hear, rather than the truth.

Not only will you have to tackle obsequious employees, but other obstacles to your business include non-payment tactics employed by your clients' accountants, such as: the cheque is ready, but it just needs the signature of someone who (conveniently) won't be in the country for weeks. Conversely, your own accountant can sabotage your business reputation by failing to release money at the right time.

Finally, you have no legal recourse if a client fails to pay you; you may even have to physically sit in a client's office to get your dues as there's no such thing as a small-claims court.

For the official information about starting a business in Dubai, see Motivate Publishing's *Dubai Business Handbook*, published on behalf of Dubai's Department of Tourism and Commerce Marketing.

Above: Dubai Internet City, which houses such luminaries as HP, Canon and Oracle.
Following spread: Working in Deira is a man's world. The glimpse of a woman will cause many stares.

HOME LIFE

Many people come to Dubai in search of a better quality of life, to save money in a tax-free environment and replace the cold dankness of home with warm, benign sunshine.

Certainly, a Dubai winter is the perfect time for outdoor living; on a par with the best in the world and, for six months of the year, it's mild and sunny on the whole, although there are strong *shamals* (winds), thunderstorms, rain and even hail the size of marbles on occasion. When the rains come, the roads will flood and it's best to have a raft of towels on standby as your apartment or villa may flood because of its non-waterproof window frames. Snow even fell in the Hajar Mountains in Ra's al-Khaimah during the winter of 2004/5, the first time in more than 40 years.

From May to October, it's extremely hot and humid; even sunglasses steam up in temperatures that can exceed 50°C, with humidity some 90 per cent and beyond.

Fortunately, air-conditioners are everywhere and Dubai's residents manage to get through the summer by leaping from one air-conditioned environment to the next.

TAX

Although there is currently no income tax in Dubai, there is Municipality Tax on property: five per cent of annual rent, or 0.5 per cent of the price of your home per year if you've bought. In addition and perhaps not surprisingly, alcohol is taxed at 30 per cent; there's five per cent tax on things like concert tickets, and 10 per cent for food and alcohol at restaurants.

Dubai Marina, a 'freehold' community of villas and apartments available for expatriates to purchase.

Although for the majority of the time Dubai is sunny, there are grim days like this.

Above: This was the temperature and humidity on Friday 28 June 2002; and it can get hotter.
Right: Garden View Villas and The Gardens with Jumeirah Beach Residence in the distance.

Interestingly, in 2005, the UAE sought technical assistance from the International Monetary Fund (IMF) to introduce Value Added Tax (VAT). According to the *Gulf News*, Dubai Customs and the IMF, in coordination with the UAE Ministry of Finance, began to take its first steps towards the introduction of VAT in February 2006, which analysts believe will affect inflation.

And, in 2006, the UAE's neighbour, Kuwait, announced it was looking at ways to introduce income tax for all residents. If Kuwait does introduce this tax, it may not be too long before the UAE and other AGCC countries follow suit.

INFLATION

According to the *Gulf News*, the National Bank of Dubai has put Dubai's inflation figure at between 15–22 per cent. The IMF, which has flagged inflation as the UAE's number one challenge, has estimated the country's inflation at eight per cent.

Dubai Marina has berthing for yachts and leisure craft, and features high-rise towers and waterfront villas with stunning views of the sea, marina and nearby golf courses.

These figures are sharply at odds with the official inflation figure of between four and seven per cent (July 2006). One of the major contributors to rising inflation has and continues to be huge hikes in house rents.

AS SAFE AS HOUSES?

Dubai lies on the Western Coastal Fault Line, in a region that experiences low-to-medium levels of seismic activity. An earthquake in neighbouring Iran in November 2005, measuring 5.9 on the Richter Scale, was felt by Dubai residents, causing widespread alarm.

Fortunately, although buildings trembled, none collapsed. According to Dubai Municipality, all buildings constructed in the past two decades have had to conform to stringent building regulations, designed to withstand the forces of an earthquake measuring five on the Richter Scale. The

government has also brought in US engineers to advise on the construction of such behemoths as Burj Dubai, a contender for the title of world's tallest building. However, it's unknown whether such massive construction efforts, focused in a relatively small area over an extended period of time, will have a cumulative effect on a city so close to Iran's major fault line.

A PLACE TO LIVE

There are more than 235,000 housing units in Dubai and 70 per cent of the population rent their homes. If you move to Dubai, you have the option to rent anywhere or buy in certain 'freehold' communities.

Regulated by Law No 5 (1985) of the UAE Civil Law (Federal), to rent a property you must have a residence visa. If you're on an expatriate package (usually if your employer is a large multinational company), your company should provide

Emirates Hills, an exclusive community of beautiful villas with a Middle Eastern flavour. Set beside an international golf course, you'll find some of the largest plots of land available in Dubai.

accommodation for you until you're legal and can find a place of you own. But, if like many others who arrive 'on spec' looking for a job, your options are limited: either stay in a cheap hotel or bunk down with friends.

Top tip: It's against the law to live with a member of the opposite sex unless you're married to them or they're part of your immediate family. In spite of this, as long as you don't bring attention to yourselves, no one cares too much.

Since 2002, when expatriates entered the property market, rents for apartments and villas have increased dramatically. The pervading atmosphere since has become one of increasing greed, which seems to grip more and more people because there are no effective safeguards to temper it. Add price increases in basic goods and services, along with wages that barely move upwards, and you're likely to find that it's almost impossible to save money in Dubai. In fact, rents have increased to such a degree that many expatriates have either left Dubai altogether, moved in with friends, moved their families back home or moved to a different emirate, such as Ajman, where rents are half those in Dubai.

Many who can't leave, especially Asian bachelors, live in their cars (although according to the police, this is illegal) and make use of what's known as 'house facilities' whereby, for between Dhs50–75 a month, they can store their luggage in someone's villa and make use of their bathing, washing and ironing facilities.

Increasing disenchantment from many of Dubai's residents in late 2005 led to calls for an end to greedy landlords and their exploitation of tenants. Reacting to this major issue, Sheikh Mohammed made a promise to tenants that

Worker accommodation was shoddy down by Dubai Creek, with several men sharing this small, grubby room. These camps have now been demolished to make way for Culture Village.

Above: One of Karama's main streets. Note the accident-damaged vehicle parked near the store.
Right: The concrete jungle of Jumeirah Beach Residence, where you can enjoy the 'lifestyle of a lifetime'.

Theme-park living in the Dubai suburb of Mirdif, a study of concrete masquerading as wood in a compound of four-bedroom villas, which cost some Dhs145,000 a year in rent.

You can rent some very nice places in Dubai . . . at a price: this three-bedroom, bougainvillea-strewn villa in the exclusive area of Jumeirah, for instance, will cost you some Dhs200,000 a year.

landlords would not be allowed to increase their rents by more than 15 per cent per year, until the end of 2006. There was a further cap in January 2007, with landlords only able to increase rents by seven per cent a year, although greedy landlords still found ways to exploit loopholes in the ruling at their tenants' expense.

Once you're in a position to get your own home and take out a year's lease, it's worth dealing with a larger real-estate agent rather than directly with the landlord or a smaller agency, as the larger agents should handle all the legalities, while ensuring you're not exploited, for five per cent of the annual rent.

If you're used to paying a monthly mortgage, renting in Dubai may come as something of a shock, because in almost all cases, you can't pay monthly. There is no Direct Debit scheme in the country at all – although in mid-2006, Dubai e-government, the Commercial Bank of Dubai and Etisalat (a UAE telecoms company) were mooting

the idea – so tenants must supply post-dated cheques to landlords, who insist on being paid with, in order of preference, one cheque (ie a whole year's rent in advance), two, three or, least popular, four cheques. You will occasionally find a landlord willing to accept six cheques, but 12 cheques are virtually unprecedented.

Don't forget to read the contract's small print and make sure your post-dated cheques cover the entire year. It's been known for smaller real-estate agencies to try and con a tenant by obtaining 12 months rent in seven. In addition, some contracts will cripple you with financial penalties if you break your lease mid way through the year.

To rent your home, you have to pay a deposit of five per cent; agent's fees of around five per cent; a refundable DEWA (Dubai Electricity and Water Authority) deposit of Dhs2,000 for a villa and Dhs1,000 for an apartment, and the annual rent in one, two, three or however many post-dated cheques you've managed to negotiate with

الصفا للعقارات

AL SAFA REAL ESTATE

A DIVISION OF MUBARAK AL SHAMSI

Email:alsafacity@eim.ae

PO Box 121324, Dubai, UAE, Tel: 04-3210588, Fax: 04-3216577

To,

Dubai, U.A.E.

Date: 10 /12 /2005

LNO: 2005, 1028

Subject: 3 B/R villas in Mirdif

Dear Sir,

We would like to conform you the above villa to following terms and conditions

1. Rent Dhs 75,000.
2. Payable in one cheque
3. 5 % commission
4. 5,000 AED security deposit(refundable)
5. All major maintenance by Al Safa Real Estate
6. DEWA includes in the rent.

SRE

AL SAFA REAL ESTATE

Al Safa Real Estate .A.E.

A letter from Al Safa Real Estate confirming a tenancy agreement, which turned out to be bogus.

the landlord or agency. The agent will also require a photocopy of your passport and residence-visa-stamp page.

Although you may have dotted the i's and crossed the t's, it pays to remain cautious. According to reports in 7DAYS in early 2006, Al Safa Real Estate ran a legitimate operation for some three years until the end of 2005, when the company was believed to have cheated more than 70 people and companies out of millions of dirhams.

CASE STUDY – PROPERTY RENTAL 1

In November 2005, before heading back to South Africa for Christmas, my friend and I found a nice new villa in Mirdif (a suburb of Dubai) through Al Safa Real Estate, which had been in operation for a few years and had rather plush offices on Sheikh Zayed Road.

The villa was still being built, but would be ready to move into on January 1, 2006. My future housemate and I went to the company's offices, as requested, to pay a security deposit of Dhs4,000 (we managed to get it reduced from Dhs5,000) and sign

the lease agreement. When we got there, we were told by a member of staff we had to pay a year's rent in advance. It is not unusual in Dubai for landlords to ask for a year's rent in advance, but not a month before you actually move in. We informed him that we would be able to give Al Safa the year's rent, but only in January when our company was able to loan the money to us. He argued with us for a while but, in the end, he had to take what we could give him. I couldn't understand why he and Al Safa were so unhappy with that.

Al Safa took our Dhs4,000 deposit, but wouldn't give us the signed lease until it received the full year's rent of Dhs75,000. We left with the agreement that we would give Al Safa the rest of the money when we moved into the Mirdif property in January 2006. In the meantime, though, we had our deposit to secure the villa.

As I was going to be in South Africa when the villa became available, my friend was going to take care of all the initial finances and move in on January 1. She tried to call Al Safa a few days beforehand to get the keys, but got no reply. She didn't worry too much as it was the festive season, so decided that she'd move in on January 2 instead.

When she still got no reply on January 2, she went to the villa to see if it was open. Everything was locked up, so she went to Al Safa's offices, only to find that the company seemed to have packed up and left in a hurry. We found out that the police were investigating the company and we weren't the only ones to have been fooled. The police had caught a couple of offenders already, who'd run the company for a few years until they found a good time to make off with tenants' money.

My friend had the chance to identify the culprits in a police line-up, but none of the members of staff we'd seen were there. She has also since appeared in court a couple of times, but nothing has come of it thus far. We doubt we'll ever get our money back and are just fortunate we hadn't given over the full year's sum. I feel for those who did. Don't ever hand over the full sum of money until you have the keys in the lock.

THE RENT COMMITTEE

The Rent Committee, founded in 1974, arbitrates in rent disputes between landlord and tenant for four days a week from Sunday to Wednesday. Dealing with some 200 cases each week – 50 each day – around 80 per cent of cases are resolved at the first hearing. Lodging a complaint is expensive – for the committee to even look at your case, you have to pay 3.5 per cent of the total rent up front. Most of the cases, 90 per cent, involve complaints made by tenants against landlords who have tried to increase rents by more than the 15 per cent (and now seven per cent) cap decreed by Sheikh Mohammed.

Investigations by the *Gulf News* revealed that landlords were able to circumnavigate the rent-cap ruling by evicting tenants who resisted rent hikes. An official stated: "Many landlords, realising they will not be able to increase rent more than the authorised limit, have filed eviction cases asking tenants to vacate whole buildings because they want to renovate them." In that way, when tenants return to the building, they are forced to pay whatever the landlord deems appropriate.

The obvious question is: Why won't the government pass an enforcable law to protect tenants against unscrupulous landlords?

CASE STUDY – PROPERTY RENTAL 2

I couldn't believe the greed and blatant lies of my Gulf States landlord. Not only had he promised faithfully in 2004 that he wouldn't raise the rent on my two-bedroom villa in Mirdif in 2005, but in both 2002 and 2003, he'd assured me in the most grovelling of terms that, in 2004, I would be able to pay, I quote: "what I wanted", because he would've paid off his home loan by then. More fool me for believing he possessed even a hint of integrity . . . I shouldn't really have been surprised when, instead of honouring his promise, he decided to raise the rent yet again, this time by a huge margin, equating to almost 50 per cent over the previous two years. Not only that, I was also faced with paying five per cent of the value of my rent in housing tax to Dubai Municipality. (Although this

had apparently been law since 1962, it was only at this point the Municipality had decided to enforce it.) And to add insult to injury, the landlord insisted I was responsible for the maintenance of his property, when throughout the previous years of my tenancy and the seven years I'd lived in Dubai as a whole, home maintenance had, without exception, been the landlord's responsibility. In fact, the only thing that hadn't risen was my salary and it was now going to be a huge struggle just to live, let alone enjoy all that Dubai has to offer.

Not believing the gall of the man, I tried to tackle him about this. He refused to speak to me. Instead he ran inside and hid behind a curtain, sending out a poor Philippino woman to act on his behalf instead. His blatant show of cowardice would have been funny at any other time. I made my points to no avail, trying my utmost to remain calm in an increasingly frustrating situation. Without resolution, I left, saying that if he didn't at least consider a reduction in the rent, then I'd be forced go to the Rent Committee for arbitration, even though I knew it would probably be a waste of time as I had little confidence in the committee. Two hours later, the Philippino woman phoned saying the landlord required me to vacate his property by the end of August, which is when my tenancy agreement expired. The only option for me was to find alternative accommodation, which, thankfully I was able to do. I pity my ex-landlord's new tenants as they have no idea what they're in for. Unfortunately, mine is not the only such case.

CASE STUDY – PROPERTY RENTAL 3

I received a letter from my landlord in mid-2006, informing me that, as property rentals had risen considerably since I took out my lease on a two-bedroom villa in The Springs the previous year, he wanted to increase the rent by 62 per cent from Dhs65,000 to Dhs105,000 per year. As it was, last year I had to get a lodger to pay half the rent, so I could afford to stay in Dubai another year. So what options were open to me now and what was the point of staying in Dubai? If I told the landlord this figure was contrary to Sheikh Mohammed's 15-

The Palm Jumeirah, the first of three palm-shaped islands that put Dubai on the international map.

The trunk of The Palm Jumeirah in early 2006, with the 'Golden Mile' of apartments taking shape.

per-cent promise, or that I'd make a complaint to the Rent Committee, he'd laugh in my face and say I must move out because he either wanted to sell the property or move his family in. He's got so many ways to get round the rent cap and get what he wants, while I have no recourse and, effectively, no rights. And the company I work for, like so many companies in Dubai, regards its staff as commodities to be exploited and thrown away when their energies are exhausted. It's not interested in retaining its staff by offering meaningful pay rises to counter rent hikes. My only realistic option was to leave Dubai and return home.

BUYING A PROPERTY

Dubai introduced 'freehold' (make sure you check out the definition of 'freehold' when considering purchasing a property) ownership on selected properties in certain communities to expatriates in 2002. To develop and manage the construction and sale of these assets, including those on the Palm Jumeirah, Dubai Marina and numerous gated communities, the government launched two property development companies: Nakheel (meaning 'palm' in Arabic) and Emaar Properties. The first Palm project, Nakheel's Palm Jumeirah, began in 2001 and was built on reclaimed land off the Jumeirah coastline in the shape of a palm tree. Aerial photographs of the fronds now reveal lines of tightly packed villas that look almost like terraces.

The Palm Jebel Ali, when complete, will be encircled by the Dubai Waterfront project. Some 50 per cent larger than the Palm Jumeirah, the development will include more than 1,000 water homes built on stilts, all linked together to form a 12-kilometre chain that, when viewed from above, spells out a verse of Arabic poetry written by Sheikh Mohammed, the modest architect of modern Dubai, which will read: 'Heed the wisdom of the wise: it takes a man of vision to write on water. Not everyone who rides a horse is a jockey. Great men rise to great challenges'.

The Palm Deira, with 41 fronds, will be as large as the city of Paris and is scheduled for completion in 2015. Other Nakheel projects include Jumeirah Islands, an inland island development of 46 islands containing 736 villas off Sheikh Zayed Road; The

Older properties are cheaper to rent than new, although require maintenance (your landlord's responsibility).

Spinneys is one supermarket chain that sells pork products. This example can be found at Uptown Mirdif.

World, 303 man-made islands lying four kilometres offshore; Jumeirah Lake Towers, Jumeirah Village, International City, The Lost City, Discovery Gardens, the vast Dubai Waterfront & Arabian Canal, The Gardens and the Garden View Villas, which consist of 208 three and four-bedroom villas built on the side of Jebel Ali, the highest point in Dubai and the site of one or two caves. Properties in the Garden View Villas appeared to have subsidence problems (see the photos on pages 96 and 97) and some purchasers who'd already moved in to their luxury homes, especially on the higher slopes, had to leave. Some 10 villas on the lower slopes are currently inhabited, but many of the higher villas are believed to be scheduled for demolition or will be rented out if deemed safe enough. The community is now a ghost town, yet the public areas, vegetation, lawns and street lighting are all still maintained, giving the impression the neighbourhood is still populated.

Emaar Properties has not been immune from its share of problems either. In early 2006, numerous Emaar villas were flooded, with residents complaining of rainwater pouring in through windows, doors, ceilings, air-conditioning ducts and light fittings. However, Emaar released a statement which said: "Staff have been on site in its communities, assisting customers, following the unusually inclement weather which has revealed some leakages and, in isolated cases, some minor flooding due to drain blockages."

Emaar has numerous construction projects under way or under its belt, including the Burj Dubai, tipped to be the world's tallest tower (the final height is a closely guarded secret, although it's likely to reach 200 storeys), at the foot of which will sit one of the world's largest shopping malls – the 2.7-million square metre Dubai Mall.

Other Emaar developments include Dubai Marina, Arabian Ranches and numerous gated communities such as Emirates Hills, The Lakes, The Greens, The Meadows and The Springs. Several palm-lined roads through these communities are in the process of being transformed from four lanes into six-lane thoroughfares.

The East Parallel Road will bisect The Springs and the West Parallel Road will run alongside the western side of Emirates Hills. Destined to accommodate the excess traffic from, and relieve congestion on, Sheikh Zayed Road, construction

Water homes built on stilts on the Palm Jebel Ali look pretty, but will they be practical?

was scheduled to begin in the first quarter of 2007 and will last nearly two years.

Jumeirah Beach Residence, hugging Dubai's southern coastline and developed by Dubai Properties for an expected 40,000 residents, boasts a beach-resort lifestyle. Unfortunately, the construction of too many skyscrapers has turned a quiet, tranquil part of Dubai's southern coastline into a concrete jungle.

Along with other multipurpose developments, Dubai Properties, a member of Dubai Holding [sic], is undertaking the construction of Culture Village, opposite Dubai Festival City on the Creek; and Dubai Business Bay, a cluster of business and residential developments which, when complete, will cover an area of some 19,500 square kilometres beginning at the head of the Creek at the Ra's al-Khor wildlife sanctuary all the way to Sheikh Zayed Road.

Dubai Holding also operates Sama Dubai, currently constructing The Lagoons on a vast area of *sabkha* (salt flats) at the head of the Creek, abutting Ra's al-Khor's wildlife sanctuary. Consisting of seven independent islands of apartment blocks and villas, and expected to be complete by 2010, The Lagoons will boast not only 'freehold' residential properties, but offices, hotels, entertainment venues and more than 50 shopping malls. The project is believed to have been designed after consultation with the Dubai offices of the World Wide Fund for Nature (WWF) and Wildlife Protection Office to ensure the integrity of the wildlife sanctuary.

Other major developers include Union Properties, which is managing the construction of retail and residential developments The Green Community, Creekside Residence and Uptown Mirdif.

DUBAI'S PROPERTY LAW

Some four years after expatriates were able to purchase property, the government announced the first in a three-part property law in March 2006. The Property Registration Law allows non-UAE nationals to legally register ownership of their 'freehold' properties in their own names. Up until the announcement, buyers only had a government promise of 'freehold' ownership.

The second part of the law came out in July 2006, listing the 23 zones open to 'freehold' ownership, including Dubai Marina, the Palms, The Springs, The Meadows, The Greens and Burj Dubai.

The third part of the law, the Condominium Law, was scheduled for the end of 2006 (but at the time of going to press in 2007, it still had not been passed) and will summarise the obligations and rights of apartment owners with regards to common areas, maintenance and utilities (which may cost you an additional Dhs50,000 per year), so that service charges can be fixed and not raised after a sale has been concluded.

Buying a property in Dubai is a unique experience in many ways. When off-plan properties became available in the early days, there were scenes of panic buying, long queues and large cash purchases from speculators who bought, sold and made huge profits. Indeed, for many after a piece of the real-estate pie, investing in overseas property has become extremely popular, certainly in the UK, with the likes of Central and Eastern Europe, South America and Malaysia (among others) promoted to potential investors. Brokers are constantly on the look out for the next big thing, but to date, have mostly steered clear of Dubai. Why? Perhaps these experts consider Dubai's property law too vague, its market too untested and, therefore, too risky a proposition at this stage to recommend to investors.

One reason many Dubai-resident expatriates have bought property, however, is to stop throwing money away on rent and, if you expect to live in Dubai for several years, or want to purchase a holiday home, it might be worth the risk.

Top tip: Another attraction for prospective buyers is the possibility of being able to obtain and renew their residence visas, although homeowners can only apply for this visa when the property has been paid for in full and the homeowner has no other visa. It's also important to note that these visas do not give owners the right to work in Dubai.

An empty villa at Nakheel's Jumeirah Islands.

BUYER BEWARE

As with many other real-estate markets in cities around the world, there are plenty of horror stories about purchasing property in Dubai, and it's easy to find stories, rumours and opinions about the progress (or lack thereof) of some developments on reputable, and not so reputable websites.

A daily scan of the country's own press at www.gulfnews.com and www.7days.ae can reveal some interesting insights and, on the Internet, you can discover several hilariously astute blogs from residents, including:
http://secretdubai.blogspot.com and
http://dubaithoughts.blogspot.com who, enjoying the honesty of anonymity, are able to succinctly expose many a Dubai idiosyncrasy.

In a letter to *7DAYS*, LS wrote of the horror of home purchase. "Let me just share the rules of the game in home purchase here: None! There are no guidelines, no transparency, no recourse. We worked with several brokers, abandoning each out

Numerous cracks can be seen on the outside walls of this villa at the Garden View Villas.

Inside, the sitting room (top) and kitchen show marked evidence of structural damage.

Emaar's The Greens: studios, one and two-bedroom apartments set along green streetscapes, private courtyards and communal swimming pools, gyms, basketball courts and barbecue areas.

The tranquil, palm-lined Springs Drive, which is being widened into a six-lane thoroughfare.

The two and three-bedroom Springs town houses are interspersed with lakes, community swimming pools, recreation facilities and numerous shopping outlets.

Villas at Emirates Hills are surrounded by the world-class Montgomerie golf course.

Discovery Gardens under construction near Jebel Ali.

of disgust at their greed (no guidelines). We 'lost' two properties because the owners reneged on their promises to sell after accepting our deposits (no regulation, no recourse). Through it all, our loan officer from a local 'reputable' mortgage lender was pressuring us to 'just simply buy anything' and, when we finally did, he took a one per cent cut from the broker! (no transparency). He threatened us when we demanded paperwork to justify the numbers (no recourse)."

In addition, numerous owners have expressed concerns about the quality of workmanship at their properties, although it doesn't bode well to lose your temper. One home owner from the US was so frustrated with one developer's lack of competence with work carried out at his property, according to *7DAYS*, that, during a visit to the developer's offices, he unleashed a torrent of abuse at a customer-service representative. Security was called, along with the police, and the American was jailed for a month and received a Dhs5,000 fine. The security guard, who swore back at the American, was also fined Dhs5,000.

House prices, along with rents, have increased exponentially in the past few years, not least because of the increasing costs of building materials. How long this can be sustained is anyone's guess. Although the government points to there being more demand than supply at the moment, a state of affairs that should ease once more development projects are completed, it's incredible the number of homes that still appear to be empty.

Before purchasing a home in Dubai, take proper financial and legal advice, conduct your own due diligence, speak to other home owners if possible (have a look at http://groups.msn. com/TheSpringsMeadowsandLakesCommunityNews to get the latest from Emaar home owners), have a healthy contempt for the hype and make up your own mind.

CRIME

Dubai feels very safe and is widely regarded as one of the safest cities in the world. Its police officers are usually courteous and generally fair, but typically appear unhurried in their actions.

Top tip: When dealing with the police, it's important to remember that your attitude is likely to decide the outcome of the encounter. If you're belligerent and threatening, however much in the right you may be, you'll end up the loser.

Expatriates living in Dubai must ensure they temper their actions to match those acceptable to an Islamic state. For example, it is illegal to make rude gestures or kiss intimately in public.

All too frequently, reports in the local press recount tales of errant expatriates who have not appreciated this fact. For example, a Tanzanian man received a six-month jail sentence for having an offensive sticker on his car and a British woman was sentenced to a month in jail for gesticulating in an offensive manner to an undercover policeman in an unmarked car. Another British national, a 26-year-old computer engineer, found himself behind bars for two days after he swore at a police officer. He was also fined Dhs2,000, which was later reduced to Dhs200 after his stint in jail. Yet another Briton, who cursed the *adhun* (call to prayer) and Islam, was fined Dhs4,000; and a man was fined Dhs2,000 for insulting the Qur'an.

Two Indians were sentenced to six months in jail for drinking alcohol and brawling over a woman in a nightclub. In addition, they were both fined Dhs5,000. A 23-year-old seamstress from the Philippines was arrested for wearing revealing clothes in public: a sheer dress that showed her underwear. An offence under the Federal Penal Code, which states that provocative dress must not be worn in public, a UAE lawyer said: "The law considers a dress a provocative one if it excites one's sexual desire. The law, however, does not incriminate a person for wearing one on the beach".

And every now and then, you'll read a newspaper report that has the ability to stun even the most hardened Dubai resident. For example, a European businesswoman, who sat cross-legged in court while attending her son's hearing, was taken to a police station for questioning when, upon being told to uncross her legs and sit properly by a policewoman, 'defamed' the policewoman by

calling her "stupid". An Egyptian journalist was cleared of assaulting a Bangladeshi driver following a road traffic accident, only to be found guilty of "calling him a bad name" for which he was fined Dhs500. And the bad name? A 'dog'. Two men went on trial for conning a policeman out of Dhs8,200 in exchange for the ability to control a magical genie. The two accused told the victim they could summon a genie for him if he paid them the money. And finally, in Ra's al-Khaimah, a UAE national was shocked to see pictures of a naked woman on his five-year-old son's pen when he turned the writing instrument upside down. The Indian shopkeeper, from whom the pen was purchased, also expressed shock and was forced to dump the whole consignment in a skip in the presence of the UAE national. Not content with jeopardising the shopkeeper's livelihood, the UAE national then made a complaint to the police.

Top tip: Never argue with a local because you could land yourself in serious trouble with the police, which could mean jail. If an argument is inevitable, however, consider crying as your best form of defence, even if you consider yourself the hardest of men . . . it can work wonders!

One Briton wasn't so lucky. He grew incensed with a group of UAE nationals who'd been fishing in the waters off Fujairah and caught a rare sailfish (on the WWF's endangered species list). When the Briton commented on the UAE nationals' irresponsible behaviour, an argument ensued. The police were called and the Briton was arrested and subsequently convicted of using abusive language. He was sentenced to six months in jail, although on appeal, the sentence was reduced by the Fujairah Court of Appeal to a Dhs1,000 fine. It's unknown whether the UAE nationals were prosecuted or not.

Yet two more Britons were sentenced to a month in jail and a Dhs2,000 fine followed by deportation for having sex in a car. Although the man and woman denied the offence, medical tests proved sex had taken place.

And in the neighbouring emirate of Sharjah, a

Arabian Ranches is a multi-million-dollar golf, equestrian and residential development, featuring some 3,850 homes, golf course, equestrian centre and polo ground.

The Green Community, with red-tiled roofs but, unfortunately, not a single solar panel in sight.

Jumeirah Beach Residence to the south of Dubai. Note the Burj Al Arab in the far distance.

The area now known as Jumeirah Beach Residence used to be a tranquil part of the city in 1998 when this photo was taken. The Hard Rock Café in the distance was the tallest building in the area.

103

Not all UAE nationals are millionaires, although they do like satellite TV. In April 2006, the government announced plans to spend some Dhs535 million to construct affordable housing for low-income nationals.

gardener from Pakistan was convicted by the Shariah Court of First Instance of the 'premeditated manslaughter' of a UAE national woman, and sentenced to death.

The punishment for drug offences is severe, although the severity of your sentence is likely to depend upon your nationality. A Pakistani woman was sentenced to death by Fujairah's Shariah Court after being found guilty of possessing cannabis with intent to supply. Meanwhile, a UAE national convicted of the same offence had his sentence reduced from 12 to eight years upon appeal.

If you're a celebrity, however, even better, as in the case of a Western music producer, who was caught with 1.26 g of cocaine in his possession when he arrived in Dubai. Although he pleaded guilty and was sentenced to four years in jail, he was pardoned because he was famous.

Another Westerner, tried after him on the same day for the same offence is now languishing in jail for four years.

You can be jailed for bouncing a cheque, with the plaintiff having three years from the date the cheque bounced to make a complaint to the police. In fact, there are so many bounced cheques that the police have a specialist department to deal with

them. Cheques bounce for a number of reasons: criminal intent or, more likely in the case of a rent cheque, your company hasn't paid you on time – again – and you don't have enough funds in your bank account to cover the amount you promised in all good faith you'd have on the day your landlord deposits your post-dated cheque in their bank.

If the landlord can't or won't sort this out for themselves for whatever reason, it's likely they'll go to the police to try and make a case against you. If this happens, a police officer will phone you, tell you a case is being prepared against you for bouncing a cheque, and ask whether you have the funds to pay. If you have, all well and good. Go down to the police station as soon as possible, with cash in hand (make sure it's cash), and wait for the landlord to show up.

Top tip: Smooth the process considerably by ensuring you're helpful, humble and non-confrontational at all times.

In the majority of cases, the landlord will be at the police station too, clutching the bounced cheque, so that you can hand over the cash in front of a police officer (who'll ensure fair play), and your

landlord can return the bounced cheque to you.

However, it has been known for a plaintiff to demand the 'suspect' be thrown in jail until they can be bothered to make an appearance, which may be several days away. This won't happen, unless you're extremely unfortunate.

If you don't have the money, and the amount is less that Dhs20,000, the police officer will order you to attend the police station with your passport, which will be confiscated until you can pay. If the amount is more than Dhs20,000 and you can't pay, you will be arrested and put before the court.

> Top tip: It's crucial you don't hand over any cash without receiving the bounced cheque in return because, at this stage, the police officer will not have put pen to paper and recorded the complaint, so an unscrupulous landlord could always make the same complaint against you within three years by presenting the cheque to another police officer at a later date. The onus would then be on you to prove you'd already settled the debt. If you couldn't, you'd have to pay again or face prosecution and possible jail.

DNA DATABASE

At the end of 2005, the government outlined plans to take DNA samples from every UAE resident, regardless of nationality, profession or status, to help the police in their fight against crime.

ID cards were introduced in July 2006, with the President, Sheikh Khalifa bin Zayed Al Nahyan, being the first recipient of the new card. If you move to Dubai, you will have to have an ID card too, which will not only contain details of your DNA, but your fingerprints too. The idea has been criticised by civil liberties groups, fearing it paves the way for a police state.

In addition, according to the *Gulf News,* Dubai Police are using HIV/Aids-testing kits to test prison inmates. They're also testing those detained at police stations prior to their remand. Costing as little as US$5, they're being used 'for the good of society' and, with 90 per cent accuracy, results are available in three to five minutes. The only police force in the world to have introduced this test (perhaps not surprisingly), a top police official has also hinted the police may now screen tourists for HIV/Aids as they arrive in the country, and deport those found to have the disease.

JAIL TIME

Unlike the West, where jail is reserved for the most serious offenders, such as rapists, murderers, or little old grannies who refuse to pay their Council Tax, it's easy to find yourself behind bars in Dubai, for swearing, bouncing a cheque or taking prescription medication.

Holidaymaker Tracy Wilkinson, a 43-year-old British grandmother, hit world headlines when she was detained in Dubai in March 2005, after she was found to have codeine – an illegal substance in the UAE – in her urine, prescribed to her in the UK for a back injury.

Although the police retained her passport, she was denied bail and languished for eight weeks in jail. She faced a prison term of up to four years if found guilty. After one hearing, Wilkinson told the *Gulf News*: "It's just horrendous . . . how they treat people here, guilty until you've proved you're innocent. What chance do you stand? I am innocent. I'd like to help other people, to warn them not to come to this country."

She was finally released after written evidence was presented to the court, evidence that could probably have taken a five-minute telephone call and access to a fax to obtain. Not surprisingly, Wilkinson vowed never to return to Dubai. The Wilkinson case is, unfortunately, not an isolated incident.

According to a *7DAYS* report in April 2007, an Indian man received life imprisonment for the possession and sale of codeine.

And the *Gulf News* reported that two Iranian holidaymakers in their 50s, who arrived in Dubai for a week's holiday, were arrested at the airport for possessing medicines containing banned substances, including pills and syrup that had been prescribed to them in their home country. They were charged with smuggling and possessing drugs for personal use, and spent seven months in jail.

Dubai operates a zero-tolerance drink-drive policy, so that if you're caught with even the merest whiff of alcohol in your system, you will spend a minimum of one month in jail. You're also likely to lose your driving licence permanently.

CASE STUDY – JAIL TIME

In July 2003, I was caught drink driving. It was during the late evening and the police, who were Yemeni, took me down to the police station. I was unlucky because the top policeman on duty told me the next day that if I'd been dealt with by a UAE national police officer, they would probably have taken me home instead of arresting me, because I'd actually fallen asleep at the wheel while waiting at traffic lights, and hadn't caused any harm to anyone. But because the Yemenis are trying to make a name for themselves, they'll book anyone for anything. I don't remember whether I was informed I was under arrest or read my rights.

Anyway, at the police station, they booked me in and then took me to another police station to take a sample of my blood to test for alcohol. I then contacted a local friend of mine and he submitted his passport for me, which meant that he took responsibility for me so I didn't have to go directly to jail. But if I hadn't known him, I would have gone straight to jail.

I arrived at Dubai Courts at 10.00am some two weeks later, and listened to my case being heard, although all the procedures were carried out in Arabic, so I didn't know what was going on.

They sentenced me to a month in jail and, as soon as they handed down my sentence, I was handcuffed and put in a cage/jail cell, set off to the side of the courtroom itself, to wait until everyone else's hearings had been heard. There were a lot of hearings that morning, so I sat in the jail cell for a couple of hours, listening to what was going on, but understanding nothing as it was all conducted in Arabic.

I was transferred into one of the jail cells underneath Dubai Courts until about 4.00pm. Then I, along with all the other prisoners convicted that day, were loaded onto the prison bus, and one hand was handcuffed to the prisoner beside me and the other handcuffed to the seat, and we were driven to the Central Prison in Satwa.

Once there, we were kitted out with prison clothes; white cotton lace-up trousers and a white, short-sleeved one-size-fits-all shirt. These clothes

Although it's an offence to wear revealing clothes in public, the law does not apply on the beach.

have a coloured stripe on them denoting the seriousness of the offence and the length of sentence you've received: green and blue are for low-category crimes, which I had, followed by yellow and then, finally, red, which is for the drug dealers and murderers etc, but those inmates were separated from the rest of us.

They usually put the green and blue stripes together, guys who've been sentenced from a couple of days, to 12 months, or a couple of years in jail. Yellow prisoners were those guys caught smoking marijuana or such like, who'd get four years in jail. However, the majority of inmates were inside for writing bad, or 'bounced', cheques.

Inside the jail are four big sheds, each one around one-and-a-half times the size of a basketball court, which are Sheikh Mohammed's converted horse stables. Each shed is just one big room with air conditioning, which houses 200 inmates. There are a total of 70 bunk beds, end-to-end, aligned in parallel rows with a metre of space between the rows. With only 140 beds, 60 inmates have to sleep on the floor. The first week I slept on the floor and was given a sort of horse blanket, which was home to some sort of parasite that kept on biting me, up and down my arms and across my stomach.

In the ablution area, just off from the main room, there are eight hole-in-the-ground loos and each one came with a hose . . . there was no loo roll. There are separate, lockable shower stalls with just a hose coming out of the wall, no shower head, and you could shower almost when you wanted, although during the day, the water was so bloody hot that you weren't physically able to do

so. There weren't separate basins, just one long trough that you could stand either side of, with individual taps.

After I'd been in jail for two or three days, some guards came round with appeal forms. I wasn't going to bother about appealing, because I'd got a month and knew I wasn't going to get any less. But I was told that if I didn't appeal, the court may think I was happy with my sentence and increase it. I appealed.

When I eventually got a bed, it consisted of a pillow and a piss-stained mattress. When I was there, there was a delivery of new mattresses and it was just like throwing a chunk of meat in among a group of hungry vultures. The cell I was in had around six Westerners out of 200 inmates, and each nationality, and colour, tended to stick

together and look after one another, and each other's stuff, because once you got a good mattress, you made sure you kept it.

Visiting days were Thursdays and Fridays, one day for male visitors and the other for female visitors, and your visitors could bring in money for you, which would go into a safe for you to draw out as you needed it. It was the same for prescription drugs and vitamin supplements; the pharmacist would keep them for you and give you them as and when you wanted them. I was quite lucky because I had a number of visitors and they brought me books and multivitamins.

Visits were conducted outside, in an area shaded from the sun. Prisoners line up in front of a barbed-wire fence and their visitors line up on the other side of another barbed-wire fence, across a

Above: Dubai's main jail in the Satwa district of the city.
Left: Purchasing six camels for Dhs10,000. If you bounce a cheque, you can end up in jail.

gap of some six feet also containing barbed wire. From there, you shout over to your visitors across the divide. It was better to stand next to someone speaking another language, because then you could concentrate, instead of picking up on the conversation of someone else speaking English.

I asked my visitors to bring me vitamin supplements because everyone in there was coughing and hacking, with many inmates not holding their hands over their mouths, so germs spread very easily in the large area of the shed, so much so that, during the last week I was in jail, I was really ill, even though I was taking vitamins.

The rest of the time, there was nothing to do except lie on our beds all day reading. We swapped books and I read seven novels while I was in jail. All the time, read, read, read. But with so much lying around, my body was getting sore and in need of exercise. Unfortunately, we weren't allowed to exercise. We were allowed outside three times a day: in the morning, afternoon and evening, but even then, everyone had to sit down, you couldn't exercise . . . the guards were constantly gesticulating at us to sit down, sit down.

The food was horrendous; I lost 10 kg in three weeks. It was just rice and slop, but some mornings we'd get a boiled egg, so I'd look forward to those days. We didn't have any cutlery and, although most people in jail were used to eating with their hands, I wasn't. So I was able to take a used phone card, crease it down the middle and make a good spoon out of it.

The one thing that you could eat was the JFC: 'Jail Fried Chicken', which we had once a week. That and the boiled egg were the only things I could eat. They did have a shop in the jail where you could buy stuff but it wasn't 'proper' food as such; it was only crisps, biscuits, cheese and cans of room-temperature pop, and cigarettes and phone cards. The shop was only open a couple of times a day, so during the time it was closed, other inmates would operate little markets at the end of their beds and sell stuff they'd bought from the shop themselves, obviously at a small profit.

It was also common knowledge that the tea was laced with bromide, to stop anyone getting horny, so I didn't drink any tea whatsoever. There were guys in there that were sleeping together and you never knew what was happening in the middle of the night. . . .

You weren't allowed to smoke inside but people did when the guards weren't there. Those that were caught were handcuffed to the fence outside for half an hour to an hour. They were held up to the fence on their tiptoes, and then handcuffed to the fence . . . you try and stand on your tiptoes for half an hour to an hour in the heat of a July day! Many people came back with their wrists just about bleeding because they couldn't do it.

I actually felt I was going to go deaf, because there were four loudhailers, one in each corner of the shed, which were going off all the time, calling prisoners to the office, or such and such prisoner would be released the next morning etc, all in Arabic of course, so you had to listen out for your name and then ask someone who could understand Arabic what the message was.

Because of this, everyone spoke at the top of their voices, so there was a constant cacophony of noise. The TV, which is at one end of the shed and mostly broadcasts Indian or Arabic channels, was never switched off, even during the night. One corner of the shed was set aside as a praying area, so five times a day, you'd have prayers to add to the general din.

There were regular fights, although we tended to steer clear of all that as much as we could. The guys that were caught fighting would go back to court and instead of perhaps serving one month in jail, they'd get an additional six months.

You couldn't talk to any of the guards because none of them spoke English and they weren't educated by any means. But generally they weren't an issue and they certainly steered clear of us because we spoke English and they didn't. So it was all too hard for them. If we wanted something from them, we had to find someone who spoke both languages to translate for us.

For every month a prisoner served, he'd get seven days off for good behaviour, so I did 23 days in total. I was glad to get out.

Dubai's main Etisalat tower, located near to the Creek in Deira.

If you move to Dubai, get used to seeing this on your computer screen.

Uptown Primary School in the Dubai suburb of Mirdif.

TELEPHONE AND INTERNET

Telecommunications services in the UAE are provided by two companies: Etisalat and the Emirates Integrated Telecommunications Company, otherwise known as Du. Landline calls to other local landlines in the same emirate are free of charge and other rates, including mobile phone calls, both locally and internationally, are far cheaper than those in other countries.

Etisalat, ranked 278th in the *Financial Times'* top 500 global companies (down from 138th in 2005) and valued at US$25.32 billion, is owned by the government. Du, established through pressure from the World Trade Organisation (WTO), is still a government organisation; 50 per cent is owned by the government, and the Mubadala Development Company and Emirates Communications and Technology (both government controlled) each hold a 25-per-cent share. The two companies are said to compete in products and services, but not prices.

While Etisalat is undertaking a major expansion drive into other countries, including Egypt, Greece, Russian, Syria and Yemen, to complement its existing portfolio of operations in Pakistan, Saudi Arabia, Sudan and, of course, the UAE, it refuses to bestow the same courtesy to other countries trying to make inroads into the UAE's telecoms sector, an issue that proved to be a major sticking point during the US–UAE free-trade talks in 2006, and a concern to the WTO.

Internet services in some parts of Dubai are provided via Etisalat's proxy server, which can block certain websites if the authorities deem the content inconsistent with the religious, cultural, political and moral values of the UAE. The Internet for those living in communities where property is available for expatriates to purchase, along with free zones such as Dubai Internet City and Dubai Media City, does not currently pass through the proxy, so any

content can be viewed, although this may change soon. Websites blocked by Etisalat's proxy include the obvious pornography, gambling and dating sites. Not-so-obvious websites blocked by the proxy include www.flickr.com (see page 112), an online photo management website; websites that censure Etisalat and those that threaten the government's telecommunications monopoly, such as VoIP websites Skype, Vonage, Google Talk and Efonica.

RAISING THE KIDS

Although there are no government statistics indicating the expense of raising a child in Dubai, an April 2005 article by Paula Le Flohic in *Emirates Woman* broke down the costs for the very first time. Parents found they would need to earn football-player salaries, just to raise their kids in the emirate. Including expenses for medical appointments, nappies, education, toys and maternity clothing, it would cost:

Conception–birth:	Dhs104,560
Birth–five:	Dhs707,000
Five–10:	Dhs1,055,000
10–17:	Dhs933,500
Total:	**Dhs2.8 million**

And two years on since that report was published, prices have risen exorbitantly.

Another consideration you have to think about when raising children in the UAE: parents can sponsor their daughters almost *ad infinitum*. However, you'll only be able to sponsor your sons until they're 18. When they reach this age, they're on their own.

SCHOOL

There are some 85 private foreign schools in Dubai, offering a range of curricula from pre-school to GCSE/high-school diploma level, including those from the UK, USA, Canada, France, Japan, India and Pakistan. Because of the hot temperatures, school times vary, but can operate anywhere between 7.45am–3.00pm. Girls are educated to the same

level as boys and free-of-charge public schools, once only available for UAE nationals, are now open to non-UAE nationals for a fee. However, competition for places is fierce and your child's placement cannot be guaranteed. Many schools won't begin the enrolment procedure until you're actually in Dubai and, prior to any place being offered, he or she must pass a battery of tests. Annual costs of schooling are as follows (in UAE dirhams): A non-refundable registration fee/deposit of Dhs2,500–4,000, followed by:

Nursery, KG1	25,000
GRADE 1	25,000 – 28,000
GRADES 2-6	28,000 – 32,000
GRADES 7–9	32,000 – 36,000
GRADES 10–11	36,000 – 46,500
GRADES 11-12	42,000 – 52,000

Top tip: These fees usually exclude transport, uniforms and other expenses. If your employer has brought you out to Dubai, make sure your contract stipulates the company will pay your school fees.

Schools are usually allowed to raise their fees by 20 per cent every three years. But, with the surge in property rental prices in the past few years, along with high inflation and fee-hike exemptions, many schools have been able to raise their fees by as much as 70 per cent. And there have been calls for this cap to be removed altogether. If this happens, schools will have *carte blanche* to charge parents whatever they like.

POST

There is no postal-delivery service in Dubai because there are no formal addresses in the UAE as such. Your address is a PO Box number in the Central Post Office building of whichever city you reside. Although there are street names popping up here and there, they are seldom used by anyone, except for one or two well-known roads such as Sheikh Zayed Road, the main highway between Abu Dhabi, Dubai and Sharjah. If you want to know where someone lives, you ask him or her to fax or email you a location map.

FLORA AND FAUNA

The desert habitat of the UAE supports a remarkable mix of wildlife, which also flourishes in the country's cities and urban areas as well, and Dubai is no exception. No sterile suburbia, there are several creatures with which to be wary, the most notable being the black widow, or red-back spider, whose numbers have swelled in recent years. Commonly seen in urban areas, they hide in secluded, rarely visited areas of the home and garden, among shrubs, under bricks and within rubbish. Although reports of spider bites appear to be rare, there was no antivenin available in Dubai until a newspaper highlighted the fact. Several ampoules were rushed into the country and are now available at hospitals.

Aquatic fauna to watch out for include jellyfish in September and October, and rays.

> Top tip: If you're wading in the sea, make sure you wear some kind of footwear, as people have stepped on what were believed to be stone fish and found themselves being rushed to hospital.

MEDICAL CARE

The UAE has comprehensive and almost free health-care facilities, although don't necessarily expect the same high standards of service you might be used to. When you receive your residence visa, you should also be issued with either a Government Health Card, which allows you and your dependants non-urgent medical treatment at government hospitals at a nominal charge, or with a private medical card. Emergency medical care in Dubai – at the government Rashid Hospital – is free for everyone and there are no restrictions.

There are numerous private clinics offering everything from laser surgery to liposuction, alhtough it's not cheap. Further information about medical care is available from *Dubai Explorer*.

HOME HELP

It's the norm to employ the services of a maid, or houseboy, who will usually hail from Asia. A number of agencies hire out staff and your maid will come to your home at times stipulated, for reasonable rates, usually for around Dhs20 an hour. However, you can employ your own maid or houseboy, but he or she is your responsibility and you must sponsor them.

They are entitled to free accommodation and it's usual for larger villas to contain small, separate quarters for this purpose. Earning between Dhs500 to Dhs1,200 a month, they are also entitled to a return air ticket to their country of origin every two years.

RAMADAN

The holy month of Ramadan occurs some 11 days earlier each year as it follows the Islamic instead of the Gregorian calendar.

It is a month of fasting, a time for Muslims to reflect, contemplate and reaffirm their faith, which they demonstrate by denying themselves food, drink and cigarettes during daylight hours. Each day, they awake early for *sohoor* prayers, and to

Red-back spiders are common inhabitants of residential areas. This one was lurking in a garage.

eat and drink before dawn, and then they desist for the entire day until sunset, when they break their fast at *iftar*. Traditionally the fast is broken with dates and water (which are usually available for free at petrol stations).

Non-Muslims are obliged to adhere to these rules in public too . . . by law. Article 313 of the Federal Penal Code states that daytime eating (including chewing gum), drinking, smoking or consuming anything that is breaking the fast in public, during Ramadan, is a criminal offence that carries a jail term of not more than a month or a Dhs2,000 fine. Those exempt from the law include pregnant women and pre-pubescent children.

BANKING

You'll find some 55 local and international banks operating in Dubai; and there are numerous Automated Teller Machines (ATM) around the emirate, several of which are drive-through, a real boon, especially during the hot summer months. Many banks offer online services, where it's possible to pay your telephone, water and electricity bills through their portals. However, banks in the UAE, as a whole, are unsophisticated and inflexible when compared to the West. For almost everything you need to set up your new life, such as renting a home, to have a phone connected, to open a bank account (in some cases), or to purchase a car, you'll need to show evidence of your residence visa, which is stamped in your passport. To obtain a loan, the company you work for must be on the bank's 'approved companies list' (generally, it must have enjoyed a good relationship with the bank and have more than 35 employees), your monthly salary must be deposited in the bank and you must lodge a cheque for the full amount of the loan with the bank in case you default in your payments. This way, the bank has the means to bounce your cheque and make a complaint to the police.

Mrs B, a Briton in Dubai, wrote a letter to *7DAYS* in mid-2006, outlining this practice against her husband who, at the time of writing, was languishing in jail. She wrote: "Through no fault of

his own [my husband] was forced out of the company he was working for. . . . Last Thursday he was instructed to go to Bur Dubai police station to meet a representative from the bank . . . he was arrested. The bank had presented a loan cheque knowing it would bounce and then filed a complaint. We are British nationals and have taken loans in the UK and have never been asked for a cheque to cover the amount borrowed. Through this practice of banks presenting cheques they know will bounce my husband has now been turned into a criminal."

CASE STUDY – BANK LOAN

I have had an account with a Dubai-based bank since 1998 and, in that year, I took out a loan over a 2.5-year period. I was able to acquire the loan because I worked for a company on its 'approved companies list'. As a responsible adult, I never missed a payment. As a responsible adult, it should not matter which company I work for, because the onus is on me to discharge my obligations, not the company for which I work.

Some time into the term of the loan, I changed jobs to a company not on its 'approved companies list'. The bank's policy was that, as I now worked for a 'non-approved' company, I was no longer capable of paying off my loan as I was now not responsible enough. The bank even insisted I obtain a guarantor, someone who would ensure I paid off the loan, or else I was obliged to pay off the full amount there and then. And yet, because I am a responsible adult, I continued to pay off my loan until it was completed.

I then began receiving regular calls from the bank's sales personnel, asking whether I wanted another loan; I turned them down, as I had no need for one. However, things change and when I did ask for another loan I was refused because I didn't work for a company on the bank's 'approved companies list', even though the bank's records must have indicated my status before all these salespeople began calling. The member of staff who dealt with me was incapable of demonstrating the slightest hint of initiative, flexibility or good judgement. The least I would have expected is to have been referred to another person for a decision to be made, based on my banking history. Instead I was insulted and humiliated. Then, to add insult to injury, the bank sent me a text message on my mobile phone, asking whether I needed a personal loan. Were they trying to really offend me or was it just sheer incompetence?

I do actually understand this 'approved companies list' policy in general terms; in the past, banks have incurred heavy losses because of unscrupulous customers who have obtained loans only to leave the country without paying them off. But should I have to suffer for their criminality, especially when I have an extremely good history with the bank? Are not individual cases considered on their merit, as they should in a customer-service-orientated organisation? What level of risk did I present, based on my history?

CASE STUDY – A BRUSH WITH THE LAW IN DUBAI

I'd lived in Dubai for seven years and had married my fiancé in the city. Working as a Marketing Manager for a large publishing company, I was committed to being in Dubai for the long term and took out a personal loan with my bank, a fairly new but forward-thinking bank in the region.

The loan for Dhs160,000 was repayable over four years and was approved, based on my monthly salary of Dhs11,000. A year into the loan and I was offered a new job with a much smaller company, with more responsibility and a monthly salary of Dhs15,000. I decided to accept but, in my naivety, I assumed that, as I had been repaying my loan without problem, and enjoyed an excellent banking history, the bank would have no problem with me making this change. Wrong.

The banks here, as I soon found out, grant loans based on the company you're working for and not on your banking history or performance with them. With less than 30 staff, my new employer was not on the bank's 'approved list of companies' (or any other bank for that matter, because they all adopt this policy). As a result, I

was told my bank account would be frozen until I had my new work/residence visa and either repaid the loan in full or provided a guarantor.

I was not in a position to repay the balance of the loan of Dhs136,000 in one lump sum and, as a responsible adult of 46, I really didn't want to be asking a friend to guarantee me, or my husband, who was in the process of changing his job and visa and wasn't in a position to help. I was quite simply outraged by the whole situation.

I wrote to the Branch Manager, explaining that, although I had changed jobs, nothing had changed and I was still in a position to honour my loan repayments. I even offered to increase the amount in my monthly repayments.

I also gave them all the documentation they requested from my new company, such as a salary confirmation letter, a letter confirming my visa was in the process of being finalised and a salary transfer letter, among others. The letter included my mobile number, a fax number and an email address. I waited to see whether this was sufficient for them.

To my horror, a week or so later I received a phone call from a policeman from Bur Dubai Police Station, who told me to come down to the station immediately with my passport, as the bank had filed a case against me.

I managed to stop myself panicking enough to explain to the very abrupt Arabic policeman on the phone that I didn't currently have my passport with me as my visa was being processed. I was then told to come to the police station the following morning with someone who was prepared to lodge their passport on my behalf. As you can imagine, this is quite a big thing to ask from someone, as their passport will not be returned until the case is settled. As my husband was out of the country at the time, I called a girlfriend who, having been through a similar experience herself, was happy to come to my rescue. We made arrangements to meet the following morning.

As soon as I composed myself I called the bank to ask why they hadn't responded to my letter or made any attempt to contact me before taking such drastic action as going to the police. I was told that someone had tried to call me on my mobile to tell me that my proposal to repay the loan without a guarantor was unacceptable to the bank and I had not responded.

As I had been spending much of my time in The Springs and Meadows, where there was little or no telephone reception, it didn't surprise me they couldn't get through.

But why, I asked, didn't they attempt to either email or fax me before going to the police. They weren't able to provide a satisfactory answer.

The following morning my friend met me at Bur Dubai Police Station with her passport. I was daunted and felt like a criminal. You're at a huge disadvantage if, like me, you don't speak Arabic, as you have no idea what's going on or being said around you. To be fair, the policemen concerned were all very nice and the procedure was fairly painless, but my friend was without her passport and I still had the dilemma of finding a way to repay my loan or finding someone to be a guarantor for three years . . . a lot to ask anyone. All of this while trying to make my mark in a new job and with my husband out of town.

I tried to speak to various managers in the bank, to no avail, so I decided that my only hope was to go right to the top and speak to the Head of Retail Banking himself. I managed to get his email address and wrote him a long letter, explaining my dilemma and disappointment with the bank. I had an immediate response from him, promising to look into the matter. He then made an appointment for me to come in and see him and, within 30 minutes of that very nerve-wracking visit, we were able to come to a satisfactory agreement.

I then met with the bank's collections department and provided them with post-dated cheques to cover the repayments (an imprisonable offence if they bounce). After this I was then given

Nurturing mangrove saplings, before planting, at Jebel Ali beach.

my release form to give to the police. My friend and I made another visit to Bur Dubai Police Station to finalise matters. She got her passport back and I was able to start getting over the whole ordeal.

THE ENVIRONMENT

According to a November 2005 report in the *Gulf News*, Dubai generates the world's highest amount of waste per capita, some 735 kg per annum, compared to an average of 710 kg in the US, 690 kg in Australia and just 300 kg in the UK.

However, Dubai Municipality's 'Keep Dubai Clean' initiative endeavours to educate residents in the use of rubbish bins, and around 12,000 people netted some 54 tonnes of rubbish at 12 sites throughout the country during a 'Clean Up the UAE' initiative by the Emirates Environmental Group (EEG).

The Municipality also operates beach-cleaning services and has some 350 Beach Cleaning Machines, similar to mechanical rakes, to combat the litter menace.

Yet while many countries throughout the world undertake recycling as a matter of course and boast heavyweight environmental watchdogs, Dubai's multinational population, blissfully ignorant of the need to protect the environment, finds it extremely difficult to dispose of their waste in a rubbish bin, let alone a recycling bin, preferring to drop it where they stand and assuming it's someone else's job to clean up after them. This attitude and lack of education is, sadly, reflected at the UAE's many heritage and scenic sites, with plastic bags, bottles and other litter liberally scattered about (see page 250).

According to the WWF, the UAE has the world's largest ecological footprint too and, as a result, the numbers of many species of wildlife have declined, victims of the UAE's building boom,

A clean beach, shade, showers and rubbish bins await visitors to this stretch of pristine Jebel Ali coastline.

hunting and trapping. Species affected include the White-Collared Kingfisher, whose numbers are estimated at less than 100. Even UN plans to protect the country's mangroves have been scuppered by irresponsible actions. However, at the beginning of 2007, the Ministry of Environment and Water announced it was preparing a code of conduct for construction companies that aims to preserve the environment during the country's development.

ENERGY

Following a study reported in the *Gulf News* at the beginning of 2006, which revealed a 22 per cent increase in greenhouse-gas emissions across the Middle East between 1990 and 2002, a top environmental expert called upon the Gulf's leaders to switch to renewable sources of energy.

And in a country with more than 300 days of sunshine a year, harnessing the power of the sun is such an obvious thing to want to do. But there's little evidence solar power has taken off in Dubai or the UAE, apart from small cells powering speed cameras on remote roads or flashing lights outside schools. When this form of alternative, environmentally friendly power is being embraced around the world, including in places that don't traditionally enjoy vast amounts of direct sunshine, why not Dubai? One expert estimates that countries such as the UAE could save some Dhs500 million every year by investing in solar power and also enjoy the added benefits of less pollution and reduced health problems, such as asthma. It's estimated that a single solar-power plant, covering an area of some three kilometres, could provide power to almost 100,000 households. Solar power is a long-term commitment and is expensive in the short term, probably one reason for a lack of this alternative power in 'transient' Dubai. In addition, little consideration for environmental issues and a lack of awareness have resulted in little demand.

The plans for 'New Dubai', to the south of the traditional heart of the city, began to be rolled out in the 21st century and, as such, planners had the rare opportunity to create purpose-built communities out of barren desert from the ground

Above: Solar power is limited to flashing lights outside schools or to power speed cameras.
Left: Experts believe development in Dubai has seriously damaged the local environment.

up; plans that could have encompassed state-of-the-art, eco-friendly facilities and technology such as solar power. Did this happen? Sadly not. Indeed, the sun-rich Middle East has no solar-powered homes at all, according to Switchpower, a Swedish company specialising in renewable energy services.

Although it's been hard work, environmental issues do seem, however, to be garnering attention, albeit slowly. The foundation stone for the first green building in Dubai was laid in early 2005 at the offices of Pacific Control Systems LLC in Dubai Techno Park. The new corporate headquarters now boasts solar air-conditioning and lighting. Education continues via the local press, with articles highlighting international companies' efforts to promote the idea of 'green' energy. However, although most people accept that renewable energy is the fuel of the future, it's the developers they need to convince.

COST OF LIVING

In the past few years, the cost of living in Dubai has skyrocketed, a state of affairs corroborated by the annual Mercer Human Resource Consulting Cost of Living Survey in mid-2007.

The survey ranked Dubai as the 34th most expensive city in the world, (down from 25th in 2006; but 73rd in 2005), a reflection of the city's inflation rate, and massive increases in such things as renting your home and school fees.

Opposite is a breakdown of possible average monthly outgoings you'll face if you move to Dubai, which do not take into account the expense of eating out, and general partying and gallivanting (all figures are in UAE dirhams):

Single person

Rent:	6,666 (on an average one-bedroom apartment costing Dhs80,000 pa)
Groceries:	2,000
Car loan:	1,500
DEWA:	500

Above: The cost of living has proved too much for a considerable number of residents, with many leaving. Following spread: Dubai Business Bay, with Sheikh Zayed Road blanketed in smog in the distance.

Municipality tax:	333 (Dhs4,000 per year on Dhs80,000 apartment)
Mobile phone:	300
Satellite TV:	170
Maid services:	320 (four hours a week @ Dhs20/hr)
TOTAL:	**Dhs11,789**

Married couple, two kids (Grade 8 and 12)

Rent:	15,830 (on an average three-bedroom villa costing Dhs190,000 pa)

Groceries:	4,000
Car loans:	3,000
DEWA:	1,500
Municipality tax:	790 (Dhs9,500 pa on a Dhs190,000 villa)
Mobile phone:	600
Satellite TV:	200
Maid services:	640 (eight hours a week @ Dhs20 an hour)
Gardening services:	250
School fees:	6,750
TOTAL	**Dhs33,560**

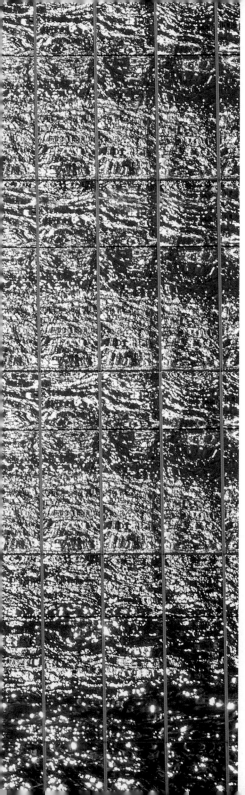

LEISURE LIFE

Dubai has become a 'Mecca' for tourism, having built an infrastructure to match anywhere else in the world ... although don't be fooled into thinking Dubai is just like the West, but with an exotic twist. The city is a rich-man's playground and a great place to come if you already have oodles of money and love a patriarchal society.

There are numerous things to do during your leisure time, from simply going to the beach and swimming in the warm waters of the Persian Gulf, to real-snow skiing in the Middle East's only real-snow ski centre.

For party lovers, you can 'arrive in style' in a hired stretch limo and get drunk every night in a different upmarket venue and not see the same place twice during the entire year, either sober or wearing beer goggles. You can pay more than Dhs20 for a glass of wine in an upmarket wine bar, while elsewhere, you can overindulge in an 'all you can eat and drink' restaurant for Dhs65.

HIP CITY

At the end of 2005, Dubai was regarded by many as the most happening place on the planet. Indeed, a report on FoxNew.com deemed Dubai as the 'Hippest City on Earth' and the most fashionable holiday destination for the rich and famous.

For those after a taste of the luxury lifestyle, and gaudy, uncouth opulence, Dubai offers it all. It is a superb place for entertainment and leisure, especially for the holidaymaker during the cooler winter months. It offers the same opulence for the Dubai resident too, especially for those lucky enough to enjoy a two-day weekend.

Hiring an abra *for a trip along the Creek is a must for new residents.*

127

On Fridays, you can often see residents relaxing on grassed areas; sometimes in the middle of roundabouts, totally oblivious to the traffic speeding past. 'Jumeirah Janes' – the lucky ladies who lunch – can be spied at Gerrard's or Magrudy's Centre over late-morning tea or luncheon, while their husbands earn enough money to pay off Third-World debt (there are nearly 60,000 millionaires in the UAE).

Everything from the sublime to the ridiculous is available in Dubai. As one expat puts it: "For Dhs30 you can get a ticket to the cinema where the film has had all the kissing cut out but, for (probably) the same price, you can get a 'hand job' from a Russian next to Golden Sands 2 (Dubai's area of closely packed high-rises near the Creek)".

However, according to the Happy Planet Index, an evalution of human well-being and environmental impact, which "addresses the relative success or failure of countries in supporting good life for their citizens, while respecting the

Above: Kitesurfing is becoming an increasingly popular sport in Dubai.
Top: Walking the dogs round one of the picturesque lakes in The Springs.

environmental resource limits upon which our lives depend," the quality of life experienced by the UAE's residents should be cause for concern, as it came a paltry 154th out of 178 countries.

PETS

Mahatma Gandhi once said: "The greatness of a nation and its moral progress can be judged by the way its animals are treated."

Unfortunately for the UAE, dogs and cats are generally unpopular among most of the country's population, even though the saluki, the Arabian desert dog, is a traditional creature alongside the camel, Arabian horse and falcon. Many are taught that dogs are impure and that black dogs are particularly evil, which is perhaps why, on occasion, children throw cans at owners and their dogs during walks.

Dubai is not geared for dogs and, in fact, can seem to work against canines and their owners:

The early evening on Jumeirah Beach is a favourite spot for a refreshing swim.

long working hours, hot weather, negative attitudes and limited, safe places to let your favourite hound off the lead for a good run all conspire against you; in fact, unleashing a dog in a public place is illegal, although as with many of Dubai's laws, enforcement rarely (but fortunately in this case) seems to happen.

However, the beach is definitely off-limits for dog walking and there are notices up everywhere warning against the practice.

As if you needed further deterrence, one tale tells of an incident several years ago, where a woman was walking her dog on the beach in the early morning. A policeman approached her, told her that dogs were not allowed on the beach, got out his revolver and shot the dog dead in front of her. How true the story is we'll never know but, unfortunately, in Dubai's anti-dog climate, it's not hard to believe.

Dog fighting is rumoured to be popular in certain circles, with stray or stolen dogs starved and tied-up outside in the heat for a few days before a fight to weaken them. In addition, many stray dogs are believed to have become a welcome meal for those desperate residents left unpaid, and starving, by the companies to which they find themselves shackled. Stray dogs lucky enough to escape these fates are rounded up and usually put down.

Dogs are despised by some so much that when a rather endearing photograph of two puppies graced the front page of *7DAYS*, accompanying a story about the local dog-rescue centre – K9 Friends – which had managed to secure shelter space for another year with the help of a dog-food manufacturer, one reader was so disgusted to be faced with pictures of dogs first thing in the morning that he actually picked up a pen and wrote in to complain.

Cruelty to animals is forbidden in Islamic Shariah and UAE laws. The UAE Penal Code states

Above: You could be risking your dog's life if you walk it on one of Dubai's beaches. Pictured is an area of beach by Jumeirah Beach Residence, with the Palm Jumeirah under construction in the distance.
Right: There are limited places to let your dogs run. This spot is in the desert adjacent to The Springs.
Page 133: Flamingos at the Ra's al-Khor wildlife sanctuary.

that any person who maliciously and intentionally kills any animal, tortures, torments, deprives it of necessary sustenance, drink or food, or cruelly beats it shall receive a prison term of up to one year, a fine of Dhs10,000, or both.

Cats don't fare much better. In mid-2006, the charity Feline Friends told *7DAYS* of the latest craze of throwing cats out of speeding cars and timing how long it took before the animal was squashed by an oncoming vehicle. In one such incident, a witness took down the registration number of a vehicle whose occupants threw a cat out at 100 kph along Sheikh Zayed Road. He reported the incident to the police, who admitted there was little they could do without at least three witnesses. Other accounts include tales of puppies and kittens being abandoned, left to die in boxes in the desert or on the side of the road in the heat of a summer's day. Many, although not all, show evidence of physical abuse.

Fortunately, in many cases, these poor animals are found and rescued by caring individuals who contact K9 Friends or Feline Friends with the intention of getting them re-homed. But, these shelters, often overflowing with other rescued dogs and cats, are often in no position to accommodate them, so the responsible finder unwittingly becomes a new dog or cat owner, without the faintest idea of how to look after it. Fortunately, the animal charities do a sterling job by helping out where they can, such as offering preferential rates for the cost of neutering, along with advice and guidance, but the task gets more difficult each year.

Dogs and cats must be vaccinated and registered with Dubai Municipality every year, and wear an identification tag or, in the case of cats, have the tip of one of their ears lopped off. Otherwise if found wandering the streets, they'll be regarded as strays. A final note on pets; although pet insurance is huge in the West, only one company offers it in Dubai: Royal & Sun Alliance.

TWITCHING

Twitchers can enjoy the birds at the Ra's al-Khor wildlife sanctuary, located at the head of the Creek and adjacent to the Al Khail Road, especially during the migration in autumn and spring. There are three hides set up for visitors, and bird life includes flamingos, storks, egrets, sand pipers, eagles, harriers, ospreys and oystercatchers among many others. This fragile eco-system, with its mangrove wetlands, abuts both Dubai Business Bay and The Lagoons currently under construction.

Ra's al-Khor sanctuary could possibly be accredited as an internationally recognised and protected wetland by the Ramsar Convention, a treaty signed in 1971 to conserve marshlands. In addition, Dubai Municipality intends to spend Dhs10 million on the construction of a visitor centre at Ra's al-Khor, to showcase the country's biodiversity and environment. The centre is expected to be ready by the end of 2007.

PARKS

Dubai boasts a plethora of parks and gardens, enclaves of greenery at the foothills of high-rise edifices. However, you should note that dogs are banned from these public areas.

One of the most established and favoured by Dubai's residents is Safa Park, which opened in 1975 and is located between Sheikh Zayed Road and Al Wasl Road. Some 64 hectares of grassed areas, trees and shrubbery provide open areas for football and secluded spots for contemplation. There's a waterfall, a lake with boats for hire, and play areas for the kids.

One of Dubai's newest parks is technology themed Za'abeel Park, opened at the end of 2005. With the high rises of Sheikh Zayed Road as a backdrop, its 47.5 hectares encompass a cricket ground, mega bowl, amphitheatre, exhibition centres, boating facilities, a restaurant, BBQ area and mini-golf. The 96-hectare Creekside Park, as its name suggests, sits alongside the Creek for some 2.5 kilometres. It boasts an amphitheatre, cable cars, a mini 18-hole golf course, restaurants and botanical gardens; and the 124-hectare Mushrif Park, located inland near Dubai's suburb of Mirdif, is an oasis among sand dunes. It contains play areas for the kids, separate

Above and top: Safa Park, opened in 1975, is one of Dubai's oldest recreational areas.
Previous spread: Za'abeel Park.

swimming pools for men and women, and lakes. One of its unique features is the International Garden Area, which features miniature buildings from around the world.

DUNE AND WADI BASHING

A favourite and time-honoured weekend pastime for residents as part of a day or overnight camping trip, a drive into the desert or mountains for dune or wadi bashing (a wadi is a river bed that, for most of the year, is dry) is something the majority of new residents are keen to try.

With cars and fuel far cheaper in Dubai than elsewhere, many expatriates can afford to buy big 4x4s, which has the added benefit of allowing their owners to sample dune and wadi bashing throughout the UAE's varied terrain. If you haven't got a 4x4, or don't want to risk damaging your own, you can book yourself on an organised off-road trip or desert safari. Many desert safaris also include an evening barbecue in *bedu* tents in the middle of the desert, camel rides and, sometimes, sand skiing.

However, if you want to use your own 4x4 to drive in the desert, make sure there are at least two cars in your party so that when (not if) you get stuck the other vehicle can pull you to safety. Carry a mobile phone with you (although sometimes you'll be out of range), enough water, sun protection, shovels and other off-roading paraphernalia, and a GPS if you have one.

Another popular sand activity is careering across the dunes in buggies, especially at the 'Big Red' sand dune on the way to Dubai's inland enclave of Hatta, where buggies can be hired by the hour.

A slow, careful drive through the wadis will reveal mountains, gorges, rocks, a multitude of plant and animal life, and an occasional rock pool and waterfall. Organised wadi-bashing trips are available and are great fun but, along with dune bashing, are not very environmentally friendly.

There are several off-roading guides available from local book shops, including *Off-road in the Emirates I* and *II*, and *Off-road Explorer*.

Dune bashing in 4x4s and buggies is a popular weekend pursuit.

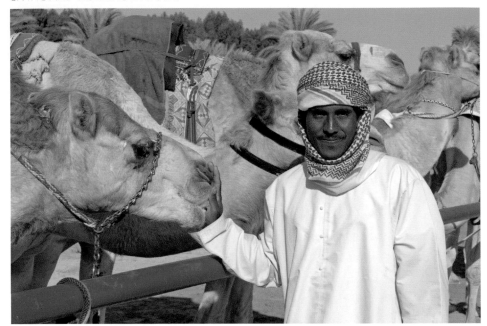

Camel racing makes for an interesting spectacle, especially with each camel and its robot jockey being pursued by a 4x4 containing the enthusiastic owner and his well-thumbed remote control.

Emirates Golf Club, with its club house shaped like traditional bedu *tents.*

Teeing off at Jebel Ali Golf Resort & Spa.

SPORT

Traditional Arab sport includes dhow racing, falconry and camel racing. Dhow racing pitted one tribe against another, while falcons were used to catch prey such as houbara and curlew to supplement a paltry diet of dates, milk and bread, with protein-rich meat. Camel racing was born from the paramount sheikh's need to test the speed and endurance of a camel he wanted to purchase, using men from his retinue as jockeys to race against each other.

The government has been quick to appreciate the lure of Western sport too, for both participants and observers alike, and it has, during the past few years, introduced more and more events to its sporting calendar. From small acorns, these events have flourished into oaks, and now attract the world's top sportsmen and women, and their fans, to Dubai. International events include the Dubai Desert Classic, part of golf's European Tour; the Dubai Open Tennis Championships, which draw interest from the top international players,

The Dubai Creek Golf & Yacht Club, with its distinctive, dhow-sail-shaped club house.

including Roger Federer, Rafael Nadal, Lindsay Davenport and Justine Henin, who have all won the championship in recent years; Dubai Rugby 7s and, of course, the 'richest horse race in the world', the US$6 million Dubai World Cup, usually won by mounts owned by the Maktoum brothers and part of a calendar of horse races taking place at the Nad al-Sheba racecourse.

However, because the UAE is an Islamic state, gambling is *haram*: forbidden. Instead, there's what's known as a 'pick six', or 'pick seven' depending on the number of races at a particular meet, whereby, before the first race starts, race goers select who they think will win each race, submit their nominations on the form provided and, at the end of the meet, winners receive cash prizes . . . all without betting any of their own money.

Other popular professional sporting activities include powerboat racing and kite surfing. Various clubs dotted throughout Dubai cater to amateurs interested in a plethora of sport, including golf, tennis, flying, go-karting, rugby, cricket, archery, football, netball and softball.

Teeing off at Nad al-Sheba Golf Club.

141

The Nad al-Sheba Golf Club and racetrack, home of the Dubai World Cup.

Above: The cricket pitch at Za'abeel Park operates regular Friday morning fixtures.
Right: A brave soul begins her descent down Wild Wadi's Jumeirah Sceirah.

And the clear, warm waters around Dubai lend themselves to the pursuit of watersports of all shapes and sizes, including snorkelling and diving, water skiing, kitesurfing, sailing and deep-sea fishing, with marlin, *hammour* and barracuda on the list of potential catches.

Indoor sport is also well catered for, and includes squash, rock-climbing, ice-skating and real-snow skiing; a real boon, especially during the summer months when it's too hot to go outside.

Dubai's latest sporting endeavour – Dubai Sports City – is part of Dubailand located next to the Emirates Road. The city, when complete, will play host to the Manchester United Soccer School (founded by Sir Alex Ferguson in 2005), the new headquarters for the International Cricket Council (ICC), which has relocated from Lord's; the David Lloyd Tennis Academy and the Butch Harmon School of Golf, along with the adjacent Dubai Autodrome and Business Park, which hosts A1 motorsport and pop concerts. The construction of this dedicated sports city has led to rumours that Dubai will bid for the 2020 Olympic Games.

LEISURE TREASURE

Wild Wadi, themed on a mythical Arab explorer called Juha and his chum Sinbad, is Dubai's water park located next to the Jumeirah Beach Hotel. It is a veritable celebration of cellulite, and you'll find all nationalities enjoying themselves, dressed in a range of attire from the skimpiest G-string bikini to fully clothed (including a veil), and everything in between. It's a superb day out for those more than 1.1-metres tall, whether they're five or 85. Operating on a cashless system where credit is loaded onto a wrist-watch type strap, which also acts as a key to your locker, more than 20 rides propel visitors round the park's 12 acres.

The Jumeirah Sceirah is believed to be the fastest and tallest free-fall slide outside the US, the end of which will leave you grovelling for your swimsuit's undercarriage; other rides include Master Blaster slides, uphill water roller coasters that pummel your bottom; the Lazy River, and the Flood River, with its surprise waves.

SHOPPING

Dubai positions itself as the shopping capital of the Middle East and boasts a range of air-conditioned shopping malls offering international brands. Yet, just as in the home rental market, rents for retail space throughout Dubai have doubled in the past year, which has led many retailers either passing on the price hikes to their customers or closing down completely.

Several of Dubai's malls are themed, such as Mercato and the Ibn Battuta Mall, designed to entertain patrons and provide a shopping 'experience'. The Mall of the Emirates, with some 450 retail outlets, even offers Ski Dubai, the city's first indoor real-snow ski resort. Even bigger will be Dubai Mall located at the foot of the Burj Dubai.

Mall hours vary from being open all day from 10.00am; from 8.00am–1.00pm and 4.00–9.00pm . . . and everything in between. The majority of larger shops outside malls are closed on Fridays, and closed during Ramadan until 4.00pm.

Haggling is expected in the souks, but shopping malls, on the whole, operate fixed prices, although some electrical shops do not price their goods until they see who wants to buy.

In early 2006, in a major coup for consumer rights, the government announced that consumers would soon be able to claim compensation for being cheated or sold faulty goods, although the ruling's robustness has yet to be tested. This was followed in mid-2006 with an announcement that the government would monitor and publish weekly prices for consumer goods, including food, clothing, construction materials and furniture, to ensure price stability.

Dubai Municipality announced a ban on smoking in shopping malls in August 2004 but, just two months later, the ruling was abandoned as it proved difficult to police. However, at the end of 2005, the UAE became a signatory to the World Health Organisation and, in January 2007, Dubai Municipality decided to try again, citing Local Order no 11 of 2003, which allows for the banning of smoking in public places to protect public health.

Although many countries have adopted the

Mercato Mall, opened in 2002, was the first Renaissance-style shopping mall in the region.

successful 'chip and pin' system when purchasing goods, Dubai has been slow off the mark, with only a small percentage of retailers adopting the system. To add to this seemingly blasé attitude to fraud and security, if you pay for your purchases using a credit or debit card, shop assistants will rarely check your signature matches that on the card as, according to a Marketing Manager from one of Dubai's major banks, it might offend the customer to do so.

At supermarket tills, there's usually a staff member who'll pack your shopping, and he or she will carry out the task with diligence and care. They'll also transfer the shopping bags to your car and it's expected to tip them between Dhs5–10, depending on the load. It's also usual for overalled men to offer car-washing services for between Dhs10–20 in the car park while you shop.

Several supermarkets sell items from the West, including pork products in designated areas. Alcohol is not sold in supermarkets, but from two suppliers, MMI and A&E, whose outlets are

The Persian section of Ibn Battuta Mall.

145

Above: Dubai's small Spice Souk is pungent and noisy, and great fun for visitors.
Top: Considering a purchase in Dubai's Gold Souk in Deira.

Arabian souvenirs are available throughout Dubai, including Madinat Jumeirah (top) and the airport (above).
Following spread: Satwa High Street, a haven for those in search of cloth and a tailor.

The indoor, real-snow Ski Dubai centre is a haven for traditional skiing and modern snow boarding. It's an incongruity in which Dubai revels and, at night, the strange-looking building is lit up by a multitude of colours.

Above, inside the Burj Al Arab's Al Muntaha restaurant, suspended 200 metres above the water; and top, the Burj Al Arab (right) stands on its own island opposite the Jumeirah Beach Hotel.

Dubailand's sales office, located near Arabian Ranches, offers a glimpse of things to come.

dotted around Dubai, usually attached to shopping centres. You require a Liquor Licence from the Police Department to purchase alcohol and it's actually illegal to purchase, or consume, alcohol without a licence. The process of obtaining a licence has been made far easier in recent years, with application forms available from MMI or A&E outlets. You need to complete the application form and, together with a passport photograph, copy of your tenancy contract, copy of your employment contract, copy of your passport with the residence-visa-stamp page and Dhs150, you can apply for an annual licence if you're non-Muslim, which is dealt with through the outlet and takes about a month to process.

However, if you don't have a residence visa, or you sublet your property from the official tenant, and are prepared to run the gauntlet of 'dry' Sharjah, there are plenty of 'holes-in-the-wall' in Umm al-Qaiwain and Ajman to choose from, including outlets at the Beach Resort hotel and the Barracuda in Umm al-Qaiwain, and a

hole-in-the-wall at Ajman Marina, opposite the Ajman Kempinski hotel. Not only is alcohol freely available to absolutely everyone, but it's also extremely cheap too; for example, a 75ml bottle of gin can cost as little as Dhs15.

However, be warned that if you're unfortunate enough to be stopped by the police in Sharjah, with alcohol in the car, you're likely to end up in jail. It's also been known for conmen to force alcohol-laden cars driven by expatriates off the road when they get into Sharjah. They're then blackmailed into handing over thousands of dirhams in return for not calling the police.

Dubai, at one time, was a haven for shoppers. It was able to offer tax-free goods at tax-free prices. Unfortunately, those days seem to have long gone, especially for luxury items which are, on the whole, far cheaper in taxed Europe or the US. However, the annual Dubai Shopping Festival, launched in 1995, still fills hotels to 90-per-cent capacity and can generate extra sales of up to US$1.5 billion.

SOUKS

Traditional local markets, souks provide Dubai with an element of spit-and-sawdust reality, and are a must see, especially with your winter visitors. Vying for space along narrow streets, the many outlets are noisy and aromatic, and vendors will engage you in conversation, offer you soft drinks, tempt you with offers to buy their spices, rugs, silks and gold among many others, and allow you to sample many of their edible wares.

According to the *CIA World Fact Book*, the UAE is a major transit hub for drugs from Asia into the West. The Brand Protection Group, based in Dubai, also believes the UAE is one of the largest transit hubs for bootlegged and illegal goods anywhere in the world, with goods entering from Asia through the country's free zones and from there, disseminating to the West.

Evidence of this litters the souks, with vendors offering an Aladdin's Cave of counterfeit watches, DVDs and handbags from secret rooms at the rear of their shops.

The Barracuda in Umm al-Qaiwain contains one of the UAE's many 'holes-in-the-wall'.

Above and right: The popular Boardwalk restaurant at the Dubai Creek Golf & Yacht Club.
Following spread: A view of Madinat Jumeirah from the top of the Burj Al Arab.

As a response to international pressure, those caught selling counterfeit goods are now arrested and deported. There's particular focus on the Gold Souk in Deira, which is a popular destination for tourists in search of a bargain.

CINEMA

Dubai shows many of the latest blockbusters – it even showed censored versions of the controversial *The Passion of the Christ* and *The Da Vinci Code* – but unfortunately, many cinemagoers' experiences are disrupted by those who refuse to turn off their mobile phones during the film. In addition, disruptive patrons will also flood the screen with scribbles of red light from their laser pens, especially during 'intimate' scenes, such as when actors of different genders hold hands.

The management are reluctant to intervene, especially when the offender is a UAE national. To add insult to injury, in late 2005, the Telecommunication Regulatory Authority (TRA) banned the use of mobile-phone-signal blocking equipment in cinemas; with premises and other businesses with the devices installed ordered to

remove them or face a prison term or a maximum fine of Dhs200,000. This strange move has led, inevitably, to reduced numbers of people visiting the cinema. In addition, the beginning of 2007 saw the price of a cinema ticket rise for the first time in many years from Dhs30 to Dhs35.

EATING OUT

There is an eclectic choice of dining options available, but for residents, Friday Brunch is a revered and much-loved Dubai institution. For a fixed price, ranging from Dhs65–Dhs395, you can seriously overindulge on real pig bacon and eggs, along with several complimentary alcoholic drinks, followed by a traditional Sunday roast, with all the trimmings; or slurp down top-brand champagne while nibbling on delicate canapés, followed by a traditional English breakfast and a Sunday roast if you've got the room. An all-day affair beginning from around 11.00am, there's often entertainment for the kids and special children's food areas, replete with small serving dishes, colourful tables and chairs and, quite often, TVs showing cartoons. For further information, see *Dubai Explorer*.

MOTORING LIFE

With just under 700,000 registered vehicles in Dubai, and with more than a million cars on Dubai's roads each day, the car is the most preferred method of transport in the emirate.

The road network around Dubai consists of between one and five lanes of traffic in each direction. Blue, green or brown signposts are written in both English and Arabic and, as the network is constantly expanding, road works are everywhere. Although many roads have names, only the well-known thoroughfares, such as Sheikh Zayed Road (the main highway between Abu Dhabi, Dubai and Sharjah) are generally referred to. Other roads have unofficial names and it's the norm for people to navigate by landmarks and location maps.

There are currently four crossing points across Dubai Creek: Shindagha Tunnel, and Maktoum, Garhoud and Business Bay bridges. A new Garhoud Bridge is currently being constructed alongside the existing bridge and will have 13 lanes. When complete in 2008, each lane will be able to carry some 2,200 vehicles an hour.

Two more lanes are also scheduled to be added to Maktoum Bridge by the third quarter of 2007; and there will be a temporary, 300-metre, floating bridge across the Creek, near the entrance to the Dubai Creek Golf & Yacht Club. With three lanes in either direction, the project is expected to open sometime in 2007.

Future plans include the widening of existing bridges to increase the number of lanes to 45 by 2008, and increasing the number of Creek crossings from the current four to seven by 2009, with the additional Fifth Bridge and Shindagha Bridge,

Sheikh Zayed Road, Dubai's most dangerous road, becomes a car park during rush hour.

Defence Roundabout. The stacked concrete wall pieces, running diagonally across the photo, used to encircle a military base (hence the roundabout's name) before being removed to make way for the construction of the Burj Dubai.

which will each boast 12 lanes.

The Roads and Transport Authority (RTA) introduced a smart traffic system along Sheikh Zayed Road in 2006, providing motorists with real-time traffic updates. It's now expected the system will roll out in other areas of the city to help reduce congestion.

Other major traffic-easing projects include the UAE's largest interchange, with three levels and 13 bridges, being built along Emirates Road at the Arabian Ranches roundabout; the widening of a 7.5-kilometre stretch of road between Garhoud Bridge and Sharjah, currently used by more than 200,000 vehicles a day; and a two-kilometre long, double-decker road on Doha Street, between the Burj Dubai and Dubai International Financial Centre (DIFC).

BUYING AND SELLING YOUR CAR

With costs up to a third less than you may be used to paying at home, and with cheap petrol, you really can purchase the car of your dreams. However, when you purchase a car, watch out for what may seem like a bargain. Your dream car may have been stolen to order from the West or been involved in an accident.

The usual method of funding the purchase of a car is through a car loan, which you'll only be able to get if the company for which you work is on your bank's 'approved companies list'. If it's not, you may be able to get finance through a dealer but, as in other countries, it usually works out more expensive than a bank loan (for more information, see *Dubai Explorer*).

If you have a bank loan and want to sell your car within the loan period, you must first pay off the loan before you transfer ownership of the vehicle. The buyer hands over funds for the car, you deposit the funds in your bank account while covering the difference (if there is any). Once the money clears, you repay your loan and the bank gives you a letter of release outlining the settlement of the loan. The only way to transfer vehicle ownership is in person. When you've got your release letter, arrange for you and the buyer to go to the Bur Dubai Traffic Police Station on Sheikh Zayed Road. Bring with you the car's registration card, your insurance certificate and lots of spare cash (to pay off your fines). Unscrew the vehicle's licence plates too. Appear lost, smile, and you'll be directed to fill out an application form. Take the form to a typing room where, for a small fee, it'll be translated into Arabic. After much to-ing and fro-ing from desk to desk, getting various bits of paperwork stamped and scribbled upon, it'll become apparent that you've finished and the transfer is complete.

DOCUMENTATION

You'll need car insurance, of course, the cost of which depends more upon the value of the car than the driving ability of the owner.

Above: An interchange along Sheikh Zayed Road near Wafi City.
Top: Dubai has expanded into the interior, as well as along the coast. Pictured is the inland Emirates Road.
Following spread: Dubai's roads generally have at least two lanes in either direction.

You'll then need to register your car. To do this, you must have the vehicle's roadworthiness checked (there are several petrol stations that double-up as vehicle-testing stations) and a valid insurance certificate. You must also pay off your motoring fines. You may be the best driver in the world, but you will inevitably accrue fines, whether for speeding, causing an obstruction or driving while talking on a mobile phone without handsfree. Fortunately, you won't receive 'black points' for any of these offences, just a fine. If you drive through a red light, which is quite a common occurrence, however, you'll have your vehicle confiscated for a week and get 12 black points. If you accrue 24 black points, you'll be banned from driving for a year.

PUBLIC TRANSPORT

Public transport is currently limited to buses; there are no railways yet, although construction of the Dubai Light Rail project has started and is set for completion in 2009. Including plans for up to seven monorails around Dubai that will link the railway to the Palms, DIFC and the City of Arabia, among others, future plans include Emirates Railway, a rail track from Abu Dhabi to Ra's al-Khaimah.

Taxis are aplenty and fares cheap. Water taxis – or *abrat* (singular *abra*) – are a traditional (albeit motorised) way of getting from one side of the Creek to the other. A one-way fare is still just 50 fils, although there are plans to raise it to Dhs1.

CONGESTION

Traffic congestion remains a huge problem in Dubai. So much so that the emirate's first toll gate system, Salik (meaning 'clear' in Arabic), opened in July 2007.

Stretching from Garhoud Bridge to the Mall of the Emirates' junction along Sheikh Zayed Road, motorists have to purchase a pre-paid card and affix a machine-readable sticker to their windscreen. As they drive along the route, they're charged Dhs4 each time they pass an electronic toll, up to Dhs24 a day.

DANGEROUS DRIVING

Despite good tarmac roads and well-maintained vehicles, Dubai's roads are some of the most hazardous. According to a 2006 UN report, the UAE's roads are the third most dangerous in the world, with 20 deaths per 100,000 population. Saudi Arabia is the most dangerous with 23 deaths per 100,000 population, and Oman second with 21 deaths per 100,000 population.

Each year, the number of deaths and serious injuries from road accidents increases, despite police efforts, including initiatives where they reward motorists who drive safely; employ mobile radar devices and increase traffic patrols. In 2005, there were 236 fatalities from road traffic accidents, involving some 300,000 vehicles (an average of some 820 a day), an increase from 206 fatalities the previous year, according to the RTA.

Figures for 2006 reveal that 283 people were killed in road traffic accidents on Dubai's roads. According to the *Gulf News*, "April and October reported the highest number of traffic deaths, with 28 deaths for each month, while November reported the lowest number of traffic deaths: 14. The two most dangerous roads in the 11 months of last year were Sheikh Zayed Road and Emirates Road with 30 deaths each".

Statistics from the Dubai Traffic Authority indicate that 97 per cent of accidents in the emirate were caused by male drivers.

With the winter rain comes even more chaos than usual. One wet February morning saw 500 accidents of varying seriousness reported before 9.00am, the result of motorists failing to adapt to the wet road conditions, speeding and not leaving enough distance from the vehicle in front. By the end of two days of rain, figures showed there had been an accident every two minutes during that period.

Ramadan tends to be another period of high accident rates. During the first three days of Ramadan 2005 for example, the number of accidents rose by almost 50 per cent to 2,313, and included three fatalities. According to one police official, the increase in the number of accidents was caused by impatience, hurrying home for *iftar* prayers, speeding and driving recklessly.

The police cite the main causes of death on the roads as reckless driving, speeding, colliding with stationary vehicles, ramming into the right side of vehicles, head-on collisions and jumping red lights. According to the Ministry of Planning, UAE nationals accounted for the majority of accident victims in 2002 (32.5 per cent), an alarming fact considering they make up only 20 per cent of the entire population.

WHY ARE DUBAI'S ROADS SO DANGEROUS?

* The majority of roads are tarmaced, smooth, more or less straight, multi-laned thoroughfares, which encourage motorists to drive at speed.
* Driving competences vary with the nationality of each driver and the standard to which they've been taught. For example, in the UK, vehicles are meant to drive on the left and use right-hand lanes for overtaking before returning to the left. Motorists in Dubai drive on the right and many drivers consider the right-hand lane as a 'slow' lane, for use by lorries only. Subsequently, many cars travel in the centre lane and, as drivers can only legally overtake on the left, this effectively reduces a three-lane carriageway to two lanes, causing traffic jams. Subsequently, motorists are obliged to 'undertake'. Confusingly, at roundabouts, many nationalities indicate left from the right-hand lane, followed by a breakaway indication to the right to go straight; some put their hazard lights on instead of headlights when it's foggy and drive slowly in the centre lane. Although UAE nationals are perceived as being 'bulletproof' when it comes to getting away with driving offences, this isn't always true. Take the case of a 17-year-old UAE national for example, who was caught driving his Lexus along Academic City Road at 200 kph (125 mph) in late 2005. He had no driving licence and, according to

Sheikh Mohammed being driven to an engagement in his Mercedes, registration number 1.

The driver of this vehicle managed to get all four wheels off the ground.

Parking is no problem in The Greens for this Jeep.

Above and left: Two silver cars fail to negotiate two different roundabouts in The Springs.

the *Gulf News*, he was arrested for performing stunts and causing a public disturbance.

- Lane discipline is non-existent, there's little to no consideration for other road users and little understanding of stopping distances, especially in wet weather.

- Although the UAE does have a version of the Highway Code, which encompasses traffic signs and road markings, rules of the road, lane discipline, U-turns, stopping distances and the correct way to negotiate roundabouts, it's not freely available to everyone. You can't buy it in the shops and, unless you're taking driving lessons, you'll probably not be aware one even exists. If you are taking driving lessons, it's likely you'll be taught how to pass the UAE driving test instead of how to drive properly. Note that if you're arriving in Dubai from a Western country, you probably won't have to retake your test, as the standard of your driving should be high enough.

- Road-traffic laws that do exist are rarely seen to be enforced by the traffic police, who command little respect because they're perceived as being reactive instead of proactive; and many of them visibly break the laws they're there to uphold. For example, one resident saw a policeman in his marked police 4x4, negotiating road works while holding his mobile phone in one hand and gesticulating at his caller with the other. In another incident reported in the letters page of *7DAYS*, 'Gobsmacked' wrote: "At 7.15 this morning, at the new traffic lights in front of

Above and top: Two accidents on Al Khail Road. 'Rubberneckers' slow traffic on the opposite carriageway.
Left: Just after a blind bend along the 'fast' lane of Dubai's most dangerous thoroughfare – Sheikh Zayed
Road – is not really an appropriate place to change a tyre.

An overturned lorry on Al Khail Road results in 'rubberneckers' getting out of their cars to watch.

Choeifat School, [I saw] a Dubai traffic police motorbike sitting at the traffic lights waiting to turn left. Traffic lights change to green, said police bike does illegal u-turn, then DOES A WHEELIE along the entire length of the school car park . . . couldn't see his number plate (due to it facing the ground at the time) but I am astonished".

- In addition, it's not uncommon to see some motorists with young children sitting on their laps, sometimes even steering the car while they pump the pedals and change gear.

With accident statistics increasing each year and no viable solution in sight, it's an unfortunate probability that you too will be involved in an accident to some degree or other.

Be aware though that procedures for minor accidents change regularly: one month you have to wait at the scene and leave your vehicle where it is or get fined; the next, you'll be fined if you don't move your vehicle out of the way, and the next month, motorists involved in a non-injury accident must go to the nearest police station to report it.

Now, minor traffic accidents are likely to be dealt with by a private company, which will free up the police to carry out more of their core roles.

And, according to a former police officer who is now a manager with the private company, staff tasked with completing accident reports will all be UAE nationals to "ensure they command the right level of respect from all drivers." Insurance companies will be charged Dhs250 for each accident report issued, with motorists ultimately footing the bill through increased annual insurance premiums.

BLOOD MONEY

If you drive, you'll be liable to pay 'blood money' (*Diya*) if, as a result of an accident, someone dies and you're to blame. *Diya* can range from between Dhs200,000–500,000 and is something your insurance company may not pay.

If this happens and you can't pay, you'll end up in jail until you can. This happened to one man

A burnt-out 4x4 abandoned on the sand along the Dubai–Hatta Road.

A car fire in the area of Garhoud is brought under control.

convicted of drink driving and the manslaughter of a Dubai resident. Although the driver was handed down a lenient four-month jail sentence, he will stay in jail until he can pay the Dhs200,000 *Diya*, which could be some years off.

An ugly phenomenon emerged in the first quarter of 2006, causing shock waves to ripple throughout the country. According to newspaper reports, several desperate, penniless construction workers tried to commit suicide by throwing themselves into the paths of oncoming vehicles, so their families could inherit the substantial *Diya*.

One Nepalese worker succeeded in his suicide bid in mid-2006, when he and an Indian colleague, both aged in their 40s, ran into the path of an oncoming vehicle being driven by a 56-year-old British resident of Dubai.

Despite braking sharply and swerving, the Briton was unable to avoid hitting the men. The Nepalese national died instantly, while the Indian was rushed to hospital. The Briton was arrested at the scene and spent more than a fortnight in jail while the police investigated the accident. Not only was he distraught at, and traumatised by, the man's death, but he was also criminalised for something that was totally out of his control; contrary to the basic premise of being innocent until proven guilty.

> Top tip: If you're a driver involved in an accident that results in injury to others, even if it's not your fault, you're likely to be arrested and jailed while the police investigate what happened.

MONEY SPINNER

In a typical month Dubai Police generates around Dhs1 million per day for the government from radar cameras, which catch nearly 110,000 motorists either speeding or jumping red lights. A new initiative was launched in early 2006, with the introduction of 32 unmarked police cars to patrol the city and put a stop to Dubai's reckless drivers. In the first 48 hours of the covert campaign, nearly one vehicle was stopped every minute for a traffic

violation; police confiscated 16 vehicles and meted out nearly Dhs70,000 in fines. Interestingly, almost a quarter of the fines were issued to motorists for driving 'outside designated lanes', otherwise known as driving along the hard shoulder.

CAR CRIME

Unfortunately, car crime is on the rise, as so many motorists park their cars and leave the engines running, especially during summer months when they want to keep the car's air-conditioning on. However, numbers are relatively low; only 161 cars were stolen while the engine was running between 2004 and May 2006.

MOBILE WHILE MOBILE

Motorists caught using their mobile phones while driving could face jail in a new initiative launched by the police. Currently, a police officer's power is limited to dispensing advice.

In another initiative, the police have launched a new SMS alert service, with motorists alerted on their mobile phones when they commit an offence.

MOTORING TOP TIPS

Advice for motorists and pedestrians trying to negotiate Dubai's roads include the following:
- Watch out for vehicles making left turns from the far right-hand lane at the very last moment.
- Don't cross the road at a Zebra Crossing. Although pedestrians may have the right of way, vehicles will not stop for you.
- Watch out for motorists stopping their vehicle in the middle of the highway to change a tyre, especially just over the brow of a hill.
- Watch out for car doors opening at traffic lights for the occupants to spit on the tarmac, an offence in the UAE. During the first half of 2006, more than 2,000 people were fined for spitting in public places. There are two offences: spitting tobacco results in a fine of Dhs500, while the even-less palatable spitting of phlegm and saliva results in a paltry Dhs100 fine.

Above: You don't wash your car yourself in Dubai as armies of low-paid workers will do it for you. Following spread: Although the roads are dangerous, many of the roadsides are well-tended.

- Also at traffic lights: in Dubai there is no amber light, so the lights will turn from red to green, followed a millisecond later by the driver behind you blowing his horn.
- For many, their two-year old child makes an excellent passenger-seat airbag.
- When taking a taxi: if the driver wants to take you round the back side, don't be alarmed; he means to drive you to the rear of the building.
- Don't trust car dealerships that fail to advertise car prices in the local newspapers. They may be waiting for you to show up and then decide the price depending on your nationality and/or gender.
- Many motorists will not drive during or after it's rained. Many taxis park up, the drivers believing it too dangerous to drive in the wet.
- When there are queues, motorists will take to driving down the hard shoulder.
- Rubbernecking is common during an accident,

which very often causes similar chaos on the other carriageway. Ghoulish motorists have been known to stop, get out of their vehicles and actually dodge across the carriageway for a better look at an accident on the other side. The police have promised to clamp down on this habit by charging motorists with obstructing the flow of traffic.

- You'll often find that the percentage of window tint is in direct proportion to the level of driving incompetence.
- For that sauna experience, especially during the summer, follow the example of many motorists by wrapping your leather seats in thick, clear plastic.
- And finally, if a 4x4, with blacked-out windows, looms large, without warning, in your rearview mirror and flashes its headlights at you, just get out of the way. Don't argue or even contemplate road rage. You'll lose.

BEYOND DUBAI

The United Arab Emirates offers a rich mix of things to do and see, from utilising state-of-the-art technology in the busiest of conurbations to stepping back in time during a stroll in the barren peaks of the Hajar Mountains, or braving the heat, emptiness and silence of the country's desert.

ABU DHABI

Abu Dhabi is the capital of the United Arab Emirates and is located on a triangular island just off the mainland. Home to more than 1.5-million people, the entire emirate covers an expanse of some 67,340 square kilometres, but only a small percentage of the territory is actually inhabited. Most of the emirate is encompassed within The Empty Quarter – or Rub al-Khali – a huge expanse of desert bordering the Sultanate of Oman, Saudi Arabia and Qatar, and made famous by the travels of Sir Wilfred Thesiger and Bertram Thomas in the early part of the 20th century.

Abu Dhabi was established in 1761, when a party of hunters from the Bani Yas confederation of tribes, ruled by Dhiyab bin Isa, the paramount sheikh from The Liwa oases on the edge of the Rub al-Khali, was believed to have discovered fresh water on the island while pursuing a gazelle (*dhabi* in Arabic). The discovery of a fresh-water source was so crucial to the survival of his tribe that the sheikh claimed ownership and established a community there, and named his new enclave Abu Dhabi, which means 'Possession of the Gazelle' or 'Father of the Gazelle' in Arabic.

The Qasr al-Hosn, or Ruler's Fort, was built in

Jahili Fort in Al Ain, birthplace of presidents.
Following spread: Al Maqta'a Bridge and the old
watchtower that guarded entry to the island.

Above: Abu Dhabi's Qasr al-Hosn, or Ruler's Fort, is open to the public.
Right: The capital's monoliths have led to the city being dubbed the 'Manhattan of the Middle East'.

Left to right: Khanzahda, Abdulla Ahmed Khan, Shahbaz, Abdul Wahkeel and Eyoub Khan from Afghanistan will sell you any number of woollen and silk rugs in their shops in Abu Dhabi's Carpet Souk near Port Zayed.

The Hili Tomb at the Hili Archaeological Gardens in Al Ain.

Above: Camels awaiting purchase at Al Ain's camel market, a popular spot for tourists.
Following spread: The modern highway snakes up Jebel Hafit, a mystical mountain of spirits.

1795, to enclose the fresh-water source. The fort also served as the home of the Ruler until 1966.

The discovery of oil following the World War II, and the inevitable wealth that came with it, began to force change upon what was a ramshackle settlement of palm-frond huts. However, the then Ruler, the ultra-conservative Sheikh Shakhbut bin Sultan Al Nahyan, was unable to cope with the rapid change and, in 1966, he was deposed by his brother, Sheikh Zayed, with British assistance. The new Ruler rushed to modernise his emirate and a grid system of high-rise, mirrored glass edifices and mosques emerged from the sand, interspersed with parks and gardens. Fortunately, the Qasr al-Hosn survived the town's renaissance.

Sheikh Zayed was determined to green the desert, so much so that Abu Dhabi became known as the 'Garden City of the Gulf'. He embarked on a huge afforestation project throughout the western part of the emirate, covering more than 100,000 hectares, and his efforts are believed to have resulted in some 140-million trees being planted.

Sheikh Zayed died in November 2004 and his son, Sheikh Khalifa bin Zayed Al Nahyan, became Ruler of Abu Dhabi, continuing in his father's footsteps, although much in his shadow, to beautify the emirate as a whole.

Not to be outdone by Dubai's Burj Al Arab hotel, Abu Dhabi opened the Emirates Palace hotel in February 2005, which is rapidly becoming one of the emirate's icons, joining the old watchtower and customs post at Al Maqta'a. In more combative times, the watchtower was manned and used to stand guard at the only crossing point (at low tide) onto the island. A causeway was built and, when Sheikh Zayed ousted his brother in 1966, the construction of Al Maqta'a Bridge began, which opened in 1968.

AL AIN

Al Ain is the Emirate of Abu Dhabi's second city, located inland some 160 kilometres from the city of Abu Dhabi. Known as the 'Oasis City' because of

Gazelles in The Empty Quarter, or Rub al-Khali.

its vast subterranean water resources, Al Ain, which means 'the spring' in Arabic, is an ancient, verdant city boasting interesting Islamic architecture and abundant modern roundabouts, yet it enjoys none of the hubbub of Abu Dhabi or Dubai, which makes a refreshing change.

Its history extends back at least 5,000 years, with Bronze Age settlements unearthed by a Danish team at the Hili Archaeological Gardens in Al Ain in the 1960s. Several flint implements have also been found at other archaeological sites, indicating an even earlier history.

Before the arrival of oil, life in Al Ain and its surroundings probably hadn't changed in centuries. Water, the most precious of commodities in the settlement's numerous oases, was able to irrigate crops and date palms by use of privately owned *aflaj* (singular *falaj*), irrigation channels that were managed by *arifs* (officials), who levied *masha* taxes for their upkeep. For their money, the farmers were allowed a certain amount of time to unblock the *falaj* and allow the water to flow into the soil around their crops.

However, oil wealth brought with it modern water pipelines, so *aflaj*, these days, are not as crucial as they once were.

Jahili Fort was built in 1898 by Zayed the Great and is one of several fortresses dotted round Al Ain. It is the birthplace of both the late Sheikh Zayed bin Sultan Al Nahyan and his son and current President of the UAE, Sheikh Khalifa bin Zayed Al Nahyan.

Al Ain is popular for its camel market, and for Jebel Hafit, the highest point in the UAE at 1,180 metres above sea level. It contains ancient tombs and is a mysterious place containing mythical *djinns* (spirits). A modern highway snakes its way to the summit, which rewards visitors with stunning views. There's also a hotel - the Mercure Jebel Hafit – along with what appears to be a palace, perched at the summit and guarded by heavy gates.

THE RUB AL-KHALI

The desert comes in a variety of forms, including vast, intricately patterned sand dunes, some more than 100-metres high, along with salt flats known locally as *sabkha*; flat, very saline expanses of crusty sand or silt created by the evaporation of sub-surface moisture.

The desert is perfect for getting away from the boisterous city and weekend camping trips are

extremely popular for groups with at least two sturdy 4x4 and a few basic survival skills. The Rub al-Khali, or Empty Quarter, in particular, is wild, unforgiving and seemingly endless, with very little flora, but abundant fauna. Sir Wilfred Thesiger was so taken with the desert's magnetic beauty that he crossed it on camel twice.

This same fascination draws intrepid visitors there to this day, although explorers must always remember to treat the desert with the respect it so obviously deserves.

FLORA AND FAUNA

Much of the emirate and, indeed, the UAE as a whole, remains a wilderness, with expanses of desert and dune as far as the eye can see. An awesome, stark sight, yet far from sterile, the desert is home to a large number and variety of creatures, including reptiles, arachnids, mammals, birds and insects.

It's quite possible you'll encounter scorpions while camping in the desert, or under rocks, debris and rubbish at home. There are believed to be some 14 species or sub-species dotted around the Arabian Peninsula and in the UAE you'll find several examples, including *Buthacus yotvatensis nigroaculeatus*, which has a yellow body, apart from the last tail segment, which is black, and can grow to some 75 mm in length; and *Androctonus crassicauda*, a black scorpion with very stout claws and a sculptured tail.

The UAE has some 17 species of snake. The majority are harmless except the Sand or Horned viper, Saw Scaled viper and Carpet viper, along with four species of highly venomous sea snake.

According to the World Conservation Union's (IUCN) Red List 2006, unless the UAE makes more effort to conserve its environment, the Hawksbill and Green turtles, Fin whale and Saker falcon are all likely to become extinct.

The number of rare, indigenous Arabian oryx continues to decline, despite the efforts of the UAE and Omani governments, which have sanctuaries containing not only oryx, but a variety of gazelles, antelope, goats and ostrich as well.

In addition, the IUCN reports that the dugong and Socotra cormorant's habitats have shrunk to such an extent they are now on its 'vulnerable' list.

The union cites hunting, animal trafficking, pollution and human disturbance through tourism as the principal causes of this decline.

Above: The Empty Quarter contains large areas of sabkha, or salt flats.
Left: Weekend camping trips in the silence of the desert are a great way to unwind.

Above: Scorpions of the UAE; left, Buthacus yotvatensis nigroaculeatus *and, right,* Androctonus crassicauda.
Below: The spiney tailed lizard, known locally as a dhab.

A Blue-headed agama, well camouflaged in the desert vegetation.

*The Purple-blushed Darter (*Trithemis annulata*) can be found patrolling the UAE's bodies of water.*

A wasp examines an egg shell for fragments of food.

The highly venomous Carpet viper poised to strike.

The UAE has two species of toad, the Arabian, Bufo arabica, *pictured, and the Dhofar,* Bufo dhofarensis.

SHARJAH

Sharjah is the UAE's third-largest emirate with
territory spanning both the east and west coasts
of the Arabian Peninsula. Meaning 'rising sun',
its history can be traced back some 6,000 years.
Latterly, Sharjah was mentioned in 1490 AD by
Ahmad ibn Majid, the famous Arab navigator.

As in the case of all the emirates, fishing,
pearling, maritime trade and tribal scuffles defined
the town in times before the discovery of oil.
The small settlement was defended by retainers
loyal to the paramount sheikh, who hailed from
the infamous Qawasim tribe, and numerous
watchtowers stand testimony to these harsh times.

Travel between the coasts was an arduous
journey, as the Hajar Mountains, known as the
'Backbone of Arabia', provided an effective barrier
to all but the most determined of travellers, who
would venture, by foot or by donkey, along dry river
beds (wadis), principally Wadi Ham from Masafi to

Above: A young camel browsing in the Hajar Mountains.
Top: The Arabian oryx remains in danger of becoming extinct throughout the Arabian Peninsula.

*Above: Gazelles (*dhabi *in Arabic) in full flight in the deserts around Abu Dhabi.*
Top: An opportunistic goat, in search of an illusive date delicacy.

197

Above: Daqiq is a large, fertile oasis fed from the perennial waters of Wadi Kitnah.
Right: Women gather reeds in Wadi Madbah, a settlement near Al Ain in Oman's Western Hajar Mountains.
Following spread: Sharjah's Husn, built in 1820, saved from demolition and now a museum.

The colour of this pool near Kitnah is almost impossibly blue, perhaps because of lime deposits.

Fujairah, or Wadi Tayyibah, from Masafi to Dibba. The journey from coast to coast could often take as long as a week to complete and it was often easier, and quicker, to sail from coast to coast.

However, with the discovery of oil came the money to blast through the mountains and construct a network of roads so that, a drive from coast to coast today takes no more than two hours.

Sharjah boasts the Gulf's first airport. Built by the British in 1932, and in service until 1977, the tiny airport served as a refuelling point for those en route from Great Britain to India and Australia. The runway survives to this day as King Abdul Aziz Street, and the control tower and hangars have been transformed into museums.

Sharjah struck oil in the emirate's offshore Mubarak Field in 1972 and the subsequent revenue bought the town a modern infrastructure.

Sharjah's modern incarnation is heavily influenced by religion and tradition. In 1998 it

Above: The Iranian Mosque, sitting on the banks of Sharjah Creek.
Right: The arch of Ibrahim Al Midfa's house and the distinctive round windtower of his majlis.

garnered the title of Cultural Capital of the Arab World by UNESCO and, to commemorate the achievement, the government erected an obelisk in the middle of the desert next to the Dhaid Road and the Arabian Wildlife Centre.

This centre is one of 20 museums and areas that venerate the emirate's heritage and traditions. Other popular museums include Ibrahim Al Midfa's *majlis* (meeting room), which contains the country's only round windtower and Sharjah's Husn. Built in 1820, the Husn, or Ruler's home, was almost completely demolished during Sharjah's race to modernise. However, at the last moment, it was saved and reconstructed into a museum.

Sharjah is the industrial powerhouse of the UAE and is the location for nearly half of the country's manufacturers. Located on the Layyah

sandspit at the mouth of Sharjah Creek on the UAE's west coast is Khaled Port, the Gulf region's busiest rig-repair facility.

In addition, in the inland, south-eastern area of the city is a 26-square kilometre industrial area. It's not a pretty sight, but a wonderful source for anything to do with cars or household furniture. There are also two main power stations at Nasiriyah and near Khaled Port on the Layyah sandspit.

Sharjah's heart has always been its natural waterways: Sharjah Creek, Khaled Lagoon and Al Khan Creek. Khaled Lagoon is encircled by an array of high-rise mirrored buildings, which sit alongside older buildings, including the Marbella Resort, one of Sharjah's first hotels, built in 1975.

One of Sharjah's most distinctive landmarks, with its blue-tiled, barrel-shaped, parallel

Sharjah fountain, in Khaled Lagoon, is one of the city's landmarks.

The elegant Sharjah Electricity & Water Authority building on the banks of Sharjah Creek.

Al Khan Creek, with the Qanat al-Qasba's distinctive Eye of the Emirates towering above.

Gargours – traditional, domed traps – festoon a dhow near the power plant on the Layyah sandspit.

Sharjah is proud to show off its heritage and traditions during festivities held throughout the year.

Above: UAE nationals perform traditional dances during a heritage festival.
Left: A traditional Arabian dhow bathed in moonlight.
Following spread: One of Sharjah's most recognisable landmarks, with its parallel, high-barrelled blue buildings and windtowers, is the Central (or Blue) Souk, which opened in 1978.

buildings, is the Central, or Blue, Souk, which was constructed in 1978 and reclines along the shores of Khaled Lagoon. Another landmark is Sharjah's fountain in Khaled Lagoon that, when switched on, shoots a continuous jet of water some 100 metres into the air.

The area around Qasba Canal, which connects Khaled Lagoon with Al Khan Creek, is one of great architectural beauty. The Qanat al-Qasba, a modern entertainment and cultural complex, encompasses modern edifices themed on traditional Islamic influences from Cordoba, Spain. Nestling within this complex is the Eye of the Emirates, the UAE's version of the London Eye, but smaller at just 60-metres tall.

Al Khan Creek, once the realm of traditional dhow yards and the site of a battle between Sharjah and Dubai in 1940, is being developed into a major entertainment area.

Sharjah prides itself on being the UAE's centre of learning and, in 1997, it opened University City, an out-of-town development of seven campuses on the Dhaid Road, which boasts architecture heavily influenced by Islam. Institutions include the American University of Sharjah, the University of Sharjah, the Higher Colleges of Technology, Sharjah Police Academy, Sharjah Institute of Technology, the College of Fine Arts and the Medical College.

Sharjah was 'Party Central' for Western expatriates living in the UAE in the 1970s and 1980s, as it offered Western entertainment and alcohol to culture-starved oil men and women.

However, extravagant construction projects and arrears resulted in discontent within the ruling family, which precipitated an attempted coup in 1987. Nevertheless, the Ruler, Dr Sheikh Sultan bin Mohammed Al Qasimi, managed to cling on to power by the thinnest of margins.

Nowadays, Sharjah is far more puritanical than its southern neighbour, Dubai, even to the point of issuing the 'Decency and Public Conduct Rules and Objectives' law in September 2001, an "invitation to everybody in the emirate, Muslims and non-Muslims, to respect decency and sublime values," according to one Sharjah Police official.

If you visit Sharjah, or pass through en route

The appetite for Western food is fully sated at Sharjah's Sahara Centre shopping mall.

Above: The Sahara Centre is also a popular venue for children to focus their after-school energies.
Right: An interesting juxtaposition between the modern Port Khor Fakkan and a traditional rowing boat.

Above: Local men from Sharjah's Khor Kalba practice for a rowing race, watched by enthusiasts.
Right: Sunset over the ancient Khor Kalba mangrove wetlands.
Following spread: The small mosque in the abandoned village of Al Jazirat al-Hamra in Ra's al-Khaimah.

somewhere else, it's important to remember that this law applies to you too, and demands you wear modest dress.

Men are forbidden from wearing shorts or exposing their chests, and UAE national men must wear more than just their *wazar* (the traditional, skirt-like undergarment) in public; women are forbidden from wearing clothing that exposes the flesh of their stomach and back; they must not wear shorts or skirts cut above the knee, and must desist from wearing tight and transparent clothing that reveals the shape of their bodies. Bathers must wear more than just a swimming costume on public beaches, although hotels and private swimming pools are excluded from this part of the law.

In addition, a man and woman should not be alone together in a public place, if they are not in a 'legally acceptable relationship', ie married, or an immediate family member. Other rules dictate dress at mosques, prohibits men from entering women-only facilities, and bars acts of harassment that violate public decency.

Sharjah's interior territory encompasses numerous acres of land set aside for agriculture, with crops of dates, vegetables and fruit being harvested on some 4,000 farms for local and international consumption.

Khor Fakkan (meaning 'creek of the two jaws') is a small town nestling around a scenic bay on the shores of the Gulf of Oman, lying north of Fujairah. Also in Sharjah's territory, Khor Fakkan is an important deep-water port, which came into its own when the first Gulf War deterred shipping from entering the Persian Gulf. Watersports are popular with residents, who can snorkel or scuba dive from the town's Oceanic hotel.

Dibba is a town divided into three. Dibba

Above: *Ra's al-Khaimah's museum is housed in the old Ruler's fort.*
Left: *A small, traditional fishing vessel moored in the still waters of Ra's al-Khaimah's mangrove-lined creek.*
Following spread: *Bithna Fort, the strategically important stronghold guarding Fujairah's Wadi Ham.*

Bayah is owned by the Sultanate of Oman, Dibba Muhallab by Fujairah and Dibba al-Hisn by Sharjah. Dibba was the scene of a huge battle between forces seeking to spread the word of Islam and those opposed to the fledgling religion, just after the death of the Prophet Mohammed in 632 AD. After the death of some 10,000 warriors, whose graves are believed to lie behind the town, the Muslim armies were victorious.

At Sharjah's southern point, just before the border with Oman, lie the 2,000-year-old mangrove wetlands in Khor Kalba, a popular destination for twitchers.

RA'S AL-KHAIMAH

The Emirate of Ra's al-Khaimah covers the country's northern territory, bordering the spectacular Musandam Peninsula of Oman. Its creek, the Khor Ra's al-Khaimah, is replete with

Above and top: Fujairah's Friday Market is a popular place to stop en route to Fujairah.
Right: A farm worker carries a crop bundle along a road in Hayl.

Fujairah Fort watches over the ruins of a settlement and its associated date-palm plantations.

beautiful, yet fragile, mangrove wetlands, which are a haven for flora and fauna.

Ra's al-Khaimah is a place rich in history. The town was previously called Julfar, and was believed to be Arabia's largest trading hub in the 16th century. Its inhabitants, including famous Arab navigator, Ahmad ibn Majid, carried out trade across the Indian Ocean and further afield, bringing Chinese porcelain, silks and spices to Arabia in exchange for incense, slaves, pearls and copper. The town of Ra's al-Khaimah, nestling at the foot of the 2,000-metre-high Hajar Mountains, was originally built to the west of its creek.

Home to the infamous Qawasim pirates, it was defended by an 18th-century fort, which also served as the Ruler's home. A bridge connects with the newer, eastern side of the town, where you'll find the modern Manar Mall shopping centre, Etisalat building and numerous government departments.

Archaeological finds date back to 5000 BC and include the round tombs of Shamal, Dhayah Fort, scene of a great battle between the British

Navy and their Omani allies against the Qawasim in 1819; and Sheba Palace.

Ra's al-Khaimah has had the same Ruler since 1948, Sheikh Saqr bin Mohammed Al Qasimi. As a result, the outlook of its population remains far more traditional than that of its neighbours.

The emirate's principal industries include agriculture, fishing, quarrying and the production of cement, a vital ingredient in the country's burgeoning property industry. Ra's al-Khaimah, although traditional, has followed in Dubai's footsteps by embracing tourism and offering property for sale on a 'freehold' basis. At the turn of the century, it opened the Tower Links Golf Course, a par 72, 18-hole, floodlit, grass golf course and academy. RAK Properties was set up by the government in 2005 to develop projects including Julfar Towers, Mina Al Arab and Mangrove Island, along with Khor Qurm, the construction of an hotel in the centre of a wildlife sanctuary.

You can now purchase one of 1,300 homes in the emirate's Al Hamra Village development, which is expected to be ready by 2007. Other resort

Bidiya Mosque, also known as the Ottoman Mosque, is the country's oldest place or worship.

developments include The Cove, covering some 50 acres of shoreline that promises its homeowners five-star luxury; Saraya Islands, a one-million square metre tourist development; and the Jebel Jais Mountain Resort, which will include a five-star hotel, cable cars, a ski slope and a falconry centre.

Al Jazirat al-Hamra, just south of Ra's al-Khaimah Town, is an abandoned fishing village that's well worth visiting, especially with winter guests. Getting out of your car and exploring the settlement will reveal traditionally built houses and an old mosque with a squat little minaret.

225

Fujairah is a popular goal for city residents who hear the weekend call of the wild.

Above: Keep your eyes peeled for petroglyphs; this example of a leopard can be found near Hayl.
Right: With the Hajar Mountains providing the perfect accompaniment, sunsets in Fujairah can be stunning.

FUJAIRAH

Fujairah is the UAE's fifth-largest emirate and it is almost entirely mountainous. The town lies on the country's east coast and is the site for one of the world's largest oil-bunkering centres. With a healthy rate of precipitation, the emirate is home to one of the country's main water suppliers at Masafi, whose bottled water is named after the village from whence it came.

With higher than average rainfall, agriculture blossoms throughout the emirate, and you'll find many examples of terraced farming cultivating such crops as alfalfa, tobacco and citrus fruit.

Fujairah Fort, reputed to be more than 350 years old, is located near the modern town of Fujairah and is encircled by the remains of a settlement and its associated date-palm plantations. It was severely damaged by British naval forces as recently as the early 20th century, but has since been restored. Another fort popular

with visitors is that at Bithna. The strategically important fort once guarded Wadi Ham, a principal route through the mountains for several hundred years before dynamite resulted in a modern tarmac road being laid.

The weekends see Fujairah come to life, with visitors from neighbouring emirates soaking up the mountains in their 4x4s, while spending the evenings camped on the beach or in wadis.

Fujairah is the place to go for the famous Friday Market, which, despite its name, is open every day. Located on the main highway between Masafi and Fujairah Town, you can buy fruit, pottery, carpets and numerous other items.

Bidiya Mosque, also known as the Ottoman Mosque, is the country's oldest place or worship. A small, square structure with four shallow domes, it squats between Khor Fakkan and Fujairah Town and comes complete with two watchtowers that provide protection from the hills above it.

Fujairah took its time to catch the tourism

Above: A devout Muslim prays in the centre of his one-family village deep in Fujairah's Hajar Mountains.
Left: A well-preserved graveyard near Wadi Sahan in the Emirate of Fujairah.

Above: Le Meridien Al Aqah Beach Resort lies on the coast between Dibba and Fujairah Town.
Top: Cooking bread on top of a metal barrel in Falakh, a hamlet in the foothills of the Hajar Mountains.
Right: Women and children, from the village of Farfar in Fujairah, come to investigate the arrival of
strangers into their community. Note the women are dressed in traditional burqa face masks.
Following spread: Umm al-Qaiwain Fort.

Above: The metal, patterned front doors to many homes in Arabia are brightly painted.
Left: Drying sardines in an area of flat desert just outside the town of Umm al-Qaiwain.

bug. It has since allowed the construction of the Le Meridien Al Aqah Beach Resort between Dibba and Fujairah Town to cater to its increasing numbers of international guests, who are keen to sample something a little more authentic than the offerings from other emirates.

Fujairah is unique in that one of its popular attractions is bull fighting; a struggle between bull and bull, and a test of strength and endurance. Fights take place during the winter months on Fridays in the late afternoon.

UMM AL-QAIWAIN

With a population of just over 62,000, the Emirate of Umm al-Qaiwain covers an area of 777 square kilometres along the country's west coast, sandwiched between Ajman to the south and Ra's al-Khaimah to the north. Inland, the emirate

stretches some 50 kilometres to the village of Falaj al-Mulla, an oasis of date-palm plantations that was once guarded by an elevated fort.

The town of Umm al-Qaiwain sits on a spit of land and, like its neighbours, was centred around a creek. Although tiny, the emirate has managed to attract visitors, with alcohol available at the Barracuda Resort and family fun at the adjacent Dreamland Aqua Park, constructed long before Dubai's Wild Wadi was even conceived; and its offering of extreme sport, including the UAQ Aeroclub, a sky-diving centre that also boasts a restaurant inside a static aeroplane; and the UAQ Shooting Club, where you can fire a range of arms from pistols to AK-47 Kalashnikov assault rifles (although it's believed this club will be closing down soon).

Sinaiyah Island, located around a kilometre offshore, is Umm al-Qaiwain's extensive wildlife

The town of Umm al-Qaiwain sits on a spit of land and, like its neighbours, is centred along a creek.

sanctuary of mangroves, which are home to numerous unique species of birds and animals. Unfortunately, in the rush to join the tourism bandwagon, these natural phenomena could disappear with the construction of the Umm al-Qaiwain Marina and its plans for more than 9,000 waterfront homes being developed by Dubai's Emaar Properties in cooperation with the Umm al-Qaiwain Government.

AJMAN

The Emirate of Ajman is the UAE's smallest at just 260-square kilometres in size. The town of Ajman, on the west coast between Sharjah and Umm al-Qaiwain, is concentrated around its own creek. The town's fort was built in the 18th century and was the Ruler's home until 1970. It then saw service as a police station and, now, it's the Ajman Museum.

Perhaps surprisingly for such a small emirate,

Ajman is the location for the world's largest dhow-building yard. Its marina enjoys sports and swimming facilities, along with a popular 'hole-in-the-wall', behind which lies the five-star Ajman Kempinski Hotel.

There's also Ajman City Centre, a modern, air-conditioned shopping mall based on Dubai's model of the same name, which houses more than 50 retail outlets, including the Carrefour supermarket, offering local and international brands.

Ajman has witnessed a construction boom in the past few years, resulting in large numbers of expatriates relocating to the emirate as more and more residents find themselves unable to afford the exorbitant rents in Dubai and, latterly, Sharjah.

Ajman has also jumped on the 'freehold' property bandwagon with the construction of various apartment blocks: Al Naeemiya Towers, Al Khor Towers, Al Rashidiya Towers and Al Corniche Tower, along with a residential and commercial

Above: The UAQ Aeroclub, a sky-diving centre in Umm al-Qaiwain, which boasts its own aeroplane restaurant.
Following spread: Ajman Fort has been the Ruler's home and a police station; but it is now a museum.

Above: Ajman City Centre offers international brands in some 50 retail outlets.
Right: A mosque silhouetted against an Ajman sunset.

development alongside the Emirates Road called Al Ameera Village. The emirate also has inland agricultural enclaves at Masfoot, near Hatta in the Hajar Mountains, and at Manama, near Dhaid.

DUBAI

Dubai's inland enclave of Hatta lies deep in the Hajar Mountains, just an hour and a half from the city centre. Hatta has been inhabited for some 3,000 years and is a popular weekend destination

for those wanting to get out of the city. Hatta Heritage Museum is a must for those who want to learn a little more about the *bedu* (local nomadic people); the popular Hatta Pools (so popular there's rubbish and graffiti everywhere) make for a good destination and to stretch the legs of your 4x4, although most of them are attainable with a saloon car; and the Hatta Fort Hotel offers Friday brunch until 11.00am, poolside eating, archery, clay-pigeon shooting, mini golf and, for tourists, camel rides.

Above: Smoking shisha *(a traditional water pipe) among the pools at Hatta.*
Right: A UAE national paddles out to read the grafitti at Hatta Pools . . . and maybe to add his own.

THE BEST AND WORST SURVEY

This small survey includes opinions from nationals of various countries, who've lived in Dubai from just a few months to several years. Although not scientific or necessarily the opinions of the author and publishers, it gives the potential new resident an idea of what to expect if they choose to live in Dubai, direct 'from the horse's mouth'.

a. Which country are you from, how many years have you lived in Dubai and what are the main things you like about Dubai?

1. South Africa. Eight months. Safety, my car and being able to use it off-road; Dubai's central location in the world and the ability to travel; my job; the social aspect (once you have a good crowd) and the food is cheap.
2. Australia. Four months. It's tax-free, exotic, shops are open late, and there are good bars and restaurants.
3. India. Two years. The lifestyle.
4. India. 11 years. Wonderful facilities, cleanliness, tax-free atmosphere, better opportunities to migrate and visit other countries.
5. Bulgaria/UK. Two-and-a-half years. Sunshine, nice sized flats, good cars.
6. Italy/UK. 10 months. Dubai is multicultural, job prospects are good, it is an excellent hub for travelling, you're able to buy an 80's Mercedes Benz SL, the extravagance and the sheer outrageousness of it all!
7. UK. Three years. The desert, the sun, the mix of people, the fun stuff to do, once you find it; the querky systems and cultural differences, even the confusion is kinda fun!
8. India. Eight years. Earlier I used to like the road network, medical facilities and other things.

Stunning flame trees in Dubai's Safa Park.

247

Not anymore though.

9. South Africa. Five years. Security, the cultural diversity and great shopping.

10. Egypt. Nearly three years. Tax-free country, clean streets and the traffic is well organised.

11. India. Six months. The quality of life that Dubai affords and the fact that, thanks to a well-networked airport, it's the gateway to so many other exotic destinations around the globe. You can make enough money here to explore other world cities.

12. Syria. I've lived in the UAE since 1974, between Abu Dhabi and Dubai, with a total of seven years in Dubai. The main things I like about Dubai are the malls, nightlife, restaurants and the friendliness of people.

13. UK. Seven years. Sunshine, good business opportunities, tax-free, high living standards.

14. UK. 11 years. Weather, living standards, low crime, golf courses.

15. UK. 14 years. Sunshine, exciting place to live, cosmopolitan, safe, good business opportunities, the sea, dancing till dawn, luxurious; and my dogs are here.

16. UK. 14 years. Weather and the relatively safe environment.

17. Australia. Seven years. Quality of life (the higher standard of general living conditions).

18. USA. Eight years. Lifestyle advantage with domestic assistance, security for your children, close friends that are like family, great restaurants and hotels, the beach and golf.

19. Canada. 13 years in the UAE as a whole. Cosmopolitan, 'happening', growing, exciting, lots of stuff to do, great restaurants, great food, gateway to many exotic destinations, lots of business opportunities.

b. What are the things you dislike about Dubai?

1. The arrogance of the some residents (particularly on the roads and in the shopping malls), the lack of culture, the lack of greenery and beauty – every beach has been spoilt by huge buildings etc; the traffic, the fact that Dubai is so dog-unfriendly, the cost of accommodation and the general mindset that the Arabs are the best beings in the world and everyone else is lower than dog shit. If only they realised that it is the expats that are keeping them in the latest fashions (under their *abayas* and *dishdashes* of course), the latest and most expensive cars and keeping the flesh on their bones. If it wasn't for expats they would still be riding camels in the desert! Perhaps that was a better life than this false, greedy Dubai we have now. Dubai is in constant denial about what's actually happening in the country – racism, child and animal abuse, slave labour, prostitution . . . the list goes on.

2. Tacky property developments, lack of an opposition government, labour conditions, poor communication systems.

3. Wages and workload . . . needs no explanation; it's quite obvious.

4. Traffic congestion and the imposition of the learning of Arabic.

5. Long working hours and low salaries in comparison to personal expenditure, no regulations with regards to housing and working. Too much traffic, discrimination, high rents/no security of investment (in case you'd like to purchase your own home), not many cultural activities, it's impossible to just jump on a plane at the weekend and go to Paris! In addition, the dirt, noise and pollution caused by continuous building.

6. Expats with delusions of grandeur who, at home, would be nothing but a geek; nationalities never really mix, even at work; the backstabbing and snitching, businesses with no real policy on employee or customer relations, which sometimes border on and cross the line at human rights' injustices; and SUVs.

7. Work/employment ethics can suck sometimes and the traffic is getting a bit much now too.

8. There's lots of racism existing in this place. Even though the British left Dubai a long time ago, the government is still a slave to the British – even locals are not as important as the Brits. Western expats (read that as white people and, most importantly, Brits) are

given top posts irrespective of whether they can deliver or not. Appearance matters a lot in the work place. It is all about marketing. Everything is superficial. They use Asians for all the hard work and credit is passed on to some Brit, South African or some other Westerner. An interesting point to note here is that you will not find a single white labourer (especially in the construction industry or in small shops) in this country. There is wide-scale disparity in wages. A Western expat is always paid more than their Asian counterpart. This treatment continues in shops, restaurants and other places. It is just assumed that if you are white, you will buy expensive stuff and if you are Asian, you are very stingy. This couldn't be further from the truth. If you notice the number of people investing in freehold properties in Dubai, you will realise that Asians easily outnumber the Westerners.

9. Building a city and a society, artificially, creates a set of problems, including a culture of greed and many uprooted individuals. My pet hate about Dubai is that everything is for 'Godda'. They are building the city at the expense (in every possible way, including finances and comfort levels) of people who are living here now, for the 'unknown' millions that will allegedly move here in 2010. I'm sure this is a well-known psychological complex, rooted in the collective psyche. Other dislikes include the high rents, traffic, living on a building site, the fact that there are no art movies, no theatre and no 'culture', there are class distinctions created with the 'haves' and the 'have nots'; you have to buy your way into whatever you want or wherever you want to go, it's a man's world, everything is for someone 'new', and tomorrow, everything will be perfect, just help us out for the next hour, the next couple of weeks, the next. . . .

10. House rent is very expensive.

11. I hate the pace at which Dubai is growing. I grew up in Dubai; I was here for the first 15 years of my life. It's like coming back home, or so I thought when I boarded the flight from Singapore to Dubai. In the years I have been away, Dubai has metamorphosed from dour to dazzling and now, it almost feels like a city that I have never been to. I am now re-exploring it and constantly looking for the Dubai I once knew. But sadly, I can only find it in my childhood albums and VHS tapes. Somehow, I can't get used to the idea. This could perhaps be attributed to the fact that I have seen a more slow, relaxed, slumbering Dubai. It's always good for a city to grow but I feel it's growing too fast and too soon, making it almost incredible. When they build so many skyscrapers, I sometimes wonder why they aren't building any skyways to get to them! The traffic situation on the ground is appalling and can put off even the most hardened global traveller.

12. Main dislikes are horrible traffic, the religious atmosphere (especially during Ramadan), the lack of freedom and, of course, the soaring prices of everything, especially houses.

13. Traffic congestion, road-traffic-accident rates, humidity, transient nature of people.

14. People are somewhat artificial, racist door policies and the slave labour of Asians.

15. Traffic, driving, paperwork, no decent jazz bar, and no decent men for my single friends.

16. Injustice to low-paid workers, over-protection of UAE nationals, abuse of house-rent increases.

17. Inability to consider permanent residence in Dubai. No reason to invest here because of this. The fact you have to leave eventually, even if it means after 20 years, because there's no choice.

18. Traffic, lack of driving ability of residents, lack of courtesy shown when queuing and parking.

19. TRAFFIC !!!

c. What are the things you wished you'd been told about Dubai before you got here?

1. How false and greedy it and its people were.

2. Nothing.

3. The truth.

4. That the rents would increase so sharply and there would be so much inflation.

5. Bureaucracy and the fact that one does not really have any rights!
6. The amount of Brits.
7. That it was gonna be a struggle to be a 'graduate' designer here.
8. That Dubai is not exactly a tax-free country. There is no tax on your income, however everything else is taxed. Indirect taxes are a common thing. Imagine paying money for the use of the airport (which prides itself as being the best in the world). Each passenger is supposed to pay Dhs30. It is one of those indirect tax things. Imagine if you have a large family. There are rumours that this figure will be increased to Dhs50. How absurd is that? Or paying housing fees to Dubai Municipality. This place doesn't give any opportunities to Asians. If you are a career-minded Asian expat then this is not the place to be.
9. Are you ready to see the worst of yourself? Are you ready to live in a place that brings forth the worst in people? Are you ready to work in a place where only what you say matters? Ready to say anything and promise anything because you never have to back it up with action or deeds? I'm glad that no one told me anything, I would never have come. I'm proud of myself for having survived here for five years.
10. That Dubai is full of prostitutes.
11. I wish I had been told that Dubai is, today, very material-driven. The city has no sentiments. No mind, only matter.
12. I can't answer that, since I've been here more or less all my life!
13. Nothing, I researched it thoroughly before moving here.
14. Things were different when I arrived here, there was nothing I would wish to be told, you respected the culture of the locals. However I don't think it's the same now. People should be told not to walk around shopping malls in strappy tops etc.
15. How much money you could make on the property market when the houses were released for sale!
16. Can't think of anything – too long ago!

17. Realistic financials of setting up in the Middle East. The cost of kids in the Middle East and the rules of having boys (if you like it here and have sons, you might want to leave well before their final years at school, because at 18 years old, they only get one-year visas and you can find your kids living somewhere else before you want them to). But mainly, you might like living here but find yourself having to repatriate much later in life . . . that's gonna be hard!
18. How to get involved with activities.
19. Nothing.

Above: Rubbish litters Wadi Hamad, near Madbah and Al Ain, in the Emirate of Abu Dhabi.
Right: Graffiti daubed on the rocks at Hatta Pools in the Emirate of Dubai.

INDEX*

* Bold text denotes subheadings

BIBLIOGRAPHY

Al Maktoum, General Sheikh Mohammed bin Rashid: *My Vision – Challenges in the Race for Excellence.* 2006

Burrowes, J: *Sultan Qaboos: The remarkable story of a king and his country.* 2006 (MS)

Codrai, R: *Dubai – An Arabian Album.* 1992

Dubal: *Dubal, From vision to reality – the first 25 years.* 2005

Heard-Bey, F: *From Trucial States to United Arab Emirates.* 2004

Henderson, E: *Arabian Destiny.* 1999

Kay, S: *Sharjah Heritage & Progress.* 2006

Naval Intelligence Division, Great Britain: *Western Arabia and the Red Sea.* 1946

Rashid, N A: *Sheikh Maktoum – Life and Times.* 2005

Rashid, N A: *Sheikh Khalifa – Life and Times.* 2007

Stannard, Dorothy: *Oman and the UAE.* 1998

Wheeler, J and Thuysbaert, P: *Telling Tales, An Oral History of Dubai.* 2005

Additional reading:
www.sheikhmohammed.co.ae

The UK's High Court of Justice judgement between Dubai Aluminium Company and Hany Mohammed Salaam and others. July 1998.

UAE – The Deira Movement. APS Review Gas Market Trends: June 24, 2002 issue.

ACKNOWLEDGEMENTS

Producing this book has been a labour of love and it is, without doubt, a project I have enjoyed immensely. It would not have been possible, however, without the help of many along the way, not least those individuals who provided case studies for the book.

In addition, I'd particularly like to thank Charlie Wright and Carmen Clews, the catalysts for my moving to Dubai in 1998; Pat McLaren, Julie Williamson and Paula Le Flohic, all ex-Dubaians who, through their input, gave me perspective and a certain degree of clarity; David Steele, my former boss and Senior Editor at Motivate Publishing, who passed on more than 30 years of publishing experience to me with alacrity and old-school dedication; Andrea Willmore, who provided me with an understanding of book design; and last but by no means least, my parents, Martin and Sonja Sanderson, without whose wholehearted support and encouragement the publishing of this book would not have been possible.

DISCLAIMER

CURRENCY CONVERTER

Dhs	£	€	US$	AUD
5	0.73	1.07	1.35	1.80
10	1.46	2.15	2.72	3.62
20	2.92	4.30	5.45	7.25
35	5.10	7.50	9.50	12.60
50	7.30	10.70	13.60	18.10
100	14.60	21.50	27.20	36.20
150	21.90	32.20	40.80	54.30
200	29.20	42.90	54.50	72.40
300	43.80	64.40	81.70	108.60
400	58.40	85.85	108.90	144.80
500	73	107.30	136.20	181
1,000	146	214.60	272.40	362
2,000	292	429.20	544.80	724
3,000	438	643.80	817.20	1,086
3,500	511	750	953	1,267
4,000	585	858	1,090	1,448
5,000	730	1,073	1,362	1,810
6,000	876	1,288	1,634	2,172

Dhs	£	€	US$	AUD
7,500	1,095	1,610	2,045	2,715
9,000	1,314	1,931	2,452	3,258
10,000	1,460	2,146	2,724	3,620
11,500	1,680	2,468	3,132	4,163
13,000	1,900	2,790	3,540	4,705
15,000	2,190	3,220	4,085	5,430
20,000	2,920	4,292	5,448	7,240
25,000	3,650	5,366	6,808	9,050
30,000	4,380	6,438	8,172	10,860
50,000	7,300	10,730	13,620	18,100
100,000	14,600	21,460	27,240	36,200
200,000	29,200	42,920	54,480	72,400
300,000	43,800	64,380	81,720	108,600
400,000	58,400	85,840	108,960	144,800
500,000	73,000	107,300	136,200	181,000
1 million	146,000	214,600	272,400	362,000
3 million	438,000	643,800	817,200	1,086,000
10 million	1,460,000	2,146,000	2,724,000	3,620,000